"I Do

"The greatest challenge for a ~~....... .. .pp.... emotionally~~ naked on the page and make that seem completely natural. Melissa Grunow does this with audacity, aplomb, and grace. Grunow illuminates 21st century issues regarding sex, body image, emotional stability, and self-realization with a fearlessness that few others can match. This is a book whose moment in history is exactly now."

—SUE WILLIAM SILVERMAN, AUTHOR OF
THE PAT BOONE FAN CLUB: MY LIFE AS A WHITE ANGLO-SAXON JEW

"In these wise essays, Melissa Grunow brings to light the hidden, the forgotten, and the discarded days. Her agile sentences and fearless gaze reveal insights that reach past easy epiphany and toward a rare clarity that is a searching delight to read."

—SONYA HUBER, AUTHOR OF *PAIN WOMAN TAKES YOUR KEYS,
AND OTHER ESSAYS FROM A NERVOUS SYSTEM*

"Melissa Grunow's *I Don't Belong Here* is a collection of deeply insightful, personal essays written with both a clear eye and a canny pen. Artfully written, the essays do almost all of the things an essay can do—there is, in the pages of this book, a master class on formalism in creative nonfiction. All of that art is brought to bear on Grunow's unsugared understanding of her life and her experiences; an understanding that is often difficult but never uncomfortable. Like all good literature, it leaves the reader with a greater understanding of what it means to be human."

—SARAH EINSTEIN, AUTHOR OF *MOT: A MEMOIR*

"Melissa Grunow's prose is a dazzling display of pathos, humor and everything in-between—like life itself. Landing somewhere between Sloane Crosley and Megan Stielstra—with a dash of David Sedaris—Grunow is a bold new voice for our time and to be savored by all. We can all see slivers of ourselves in varying degrees throughout these pages. For better and for worse."

—R.J. FOX, AUTHOR OF *AWAITING IDENTIFICATION, LOVE & VODKA: MY
SURREAL ADVENTURES IN UKRAINE,* AND *TALES FROM THE DORK SIDE*

"With disarming candor and unflinching excavation of self, Grunow has crafted a remarkable meditation on the concept of home. Her memoir plumbs our need for belonging in our structures, our communities, our professions, our relationships, and pivotally, our skins. This is a stand-out, coming-of-age tale for all of us who are discovering that 'growing up' is a lifetime endeavor."

—TABITHA BLANKENBILLER, AUTHOR OF *EATS OF EDEN: A FOODOIR*

"Melissa Grunow is a survivor. The essays in *I Don't Belong Here* sing with a fierce and hard-won wisdom. In "Before and After," Grunow writes, "Sometimes the world is one fire. Sometimes the world is under water." Her sharp-eyed prose charts a course between these worlds, delivering us through pain and loss into a place of her own making, a place in the sun."

—SUSAN MCCARTY, AUTHOR OF *ANATOMIES*

"In *I Don't Belong Here*, Grunow turns her unflinching lens on the countless steps we take away from ourselves in an effort to form human connections, even closing our eyes to the way familiarity masquerades as love. Without remorse or self-pity, she shows how we cry, curse, and claw our way back, her lyrical prose an anthem to forging her rightful place in her own life."

—ANGELA AMMAN, AUTHOR OF *NOTHING GOES AWAY: SHORT STORIES*

"Betrayed, beset, harried, and persecuted—to be female. This work stands testament to the war on women, where they are surrounded but enduring and winning the fight."

—JASON ARMENT, AUTHOR OF *MUSALAHEEN*

"In these honest, moving essays, Melissa Grunow bravely confronts 'the woolly mammoth' of fear and mental illness and recovery. Reading these fiercely candid and endearing essays made me even more convinced that speaking one's truth is *always* the best response."

—KELLY FORDON, AUTHOR OF *GARDEN FOR THE BLIND*

"Intimate. Beautifully written. Honest. Melissa Grunow's essays are written with such a personal finesse that at times it feels as though you've stumbled upon private writings. Her fearlessness is captivating and addicting."

—BRYCE DAVID SALAZAR, AUTHOR OF
SHE SEES METAPHORS AND TALES OF TIMELESS SPRINGS

"These incisive essays hover on the border of escape and endurance. Melissa Grunow explores the essential yearnings we all carry with us, even when we tell ourselves we can leave them behind and start over."

—LEIGH STEIN, AUTHOR OF *LAND OF ENCHANTMENT*

"Reading these essays is like grabbing a drink with a dear friend for a much-needed session of tender friendship, brutal frankness, and fixing old wounds. Grunow's courageous vulnerability vibrates through this book."

—MING HOLDEN, AUTHOR OF *REFUGE*

I Don't Belong Here

I Don't Belong Here

essays

MELISSA GRUNOW

LIBRARY OF CONGRESS CATALOGING-IN-PUBLICATION DATA

I Don't Belong Here
Authored by Melissa Grunow

ISBN: 9780997603897
LCCN: 2018935806

For Janel

CONTENTS

I don't care if it hurts,
I want to have control,
I want a perfect body,
I want a perfect soul,
I want you to notice,
When I'm not around,
You're so fucking special,
You're so very special,
I wish I was special.

But I'm a creep, I'm a weirdo,
What the hell am I doing here?
I don't belong here.

—RADIOHEAD, "CREEP"

PART 1
UNSPOKEN

SILENT, STIFLED LOVE

*"You cannot swim for new horizons until you
have courage to lose sight of the shore."*
—WILLIAM FAULKNER, *OLD MAN*

Hike down the hill with coolers full of beer and Jello shots; up ahead, tan bodies jiggle beneath thin bathing suits. Wade into the water up to your thighs and feel the pebbles wedge between your toes as they squish into wet sand. Hoist into canoes two-by-two and paddle. Push off boulders—icebergs of the shallow water—lean into currents and river bends, cheer and shout, "Ahoy!" Tie together a barge and pass around a fifth.

Sunscreen sizzles on your skin from the summer heat. Grip a cool can and pull back the tab; savor the *crack* as aluminum breaks apart. Bring the opening to your lips and swallow. Repeat until all the cans are depleted, the empty containers rolling around on the floor of the canoe.

He runs his fingers across your skin and unties the strings, laughing. "Always double-knot," he says. His hand lingers on your back, arms, and hips. Your fingers interlace. Know his name but not much else.

Slide forward onto his chest—blame the rocking canoe—mouth lands on mouth. It's a moment, only a moment. There are forty other people here. *And yet this—*

Pull away and regret the haste, the distance. He leans back and props his feet onto your bent knees as though there is nothing to make of it. Caress his ankle with a circling thumb and pretend to take in the changing scenery; regret that your cooler is empty.

Drag the canoe onto the beach and climb the hill. As you approach camp, exchange a smile. Unzip the tent and follow him inside. Mouth on mouth, mouth on skin, mouth on heat, eyes linger on eyes. Fingertips trace freckles, head against chest, bodies rise and fall together. Silent, stifled love.

Rain comes on strong and soaks the tent's fabric, *thunk-thunk-thunk*. Water-resistant doesn't mean water-proof. Puddles collect among the dry pine needles and dead grass as your bodies settle into the thin cushioning of the sleeping bag, still intertwined.

Leave when it's dark. He sleeps. Don't speak again.

KISSING GINGER

*"'It was a mistake,' you said. But the cruel thing was,
it felt like the mistake was mine, for trusting you."*
—DAVID LEVITHAN, *THE LOVER'S DICTIONARY*

You made a joke about the seven dwarves or the three bears or some other reference to multiple people in a bed. I probably laughed as I felt the white down duvet against my cheek and the weight on the mattress from the bodies around me. The party continued on the other side of the door, but it was getting quieter. Eliza relentlessly dialed the stereo volume knob downward out of courtesy to her neighbors who—thankfully—hadn't called the police on us. Not yet, anyway.

Earlier, someone had put the *Flashdance* soundtrack in the CD player, and I rolled around on the floor, drunk, imagining I was Jennifer Beals writhing to "What a Feeling." I didn't feel fat, tired, burned out, or anxious about finding a job now that I was graduating, even though I was all of those things. I just danced and people cheered, and when I looked around the room for you after the song was over, you weren't there.

I found you stretched out the wrong way across Eric and Eliza's bed. You smiled when you felt me flop down next to you. I probably smiled back and said something about closing my eyes for a minute, just a minute, because the bed was *so* comfortable, and I was *so* tired, and my thesis was written, submitted, approved, bound, and defended, and what if no one ever read another word I wrote?

Others came into the room and crawled in on either side of us until we made six. Their eyes fluttered closed, the vodka or wine or beer pushing them—us—into oblivion. That was when you made your joke about the bed, the one that was funny, the one where I probably laughed.

My head turned toward you and my eyelids raised slightly, then closed again, opened, then closed, then opened long enough to see Ginger, the lesbian poetry student with a pierced lip, kissing you, long enough to see you kissing her back. Then my eyes slammed shut, my hands moved to cradle my face, and I snagged the prong of my wedding ring on the duvet cover, tugging a thread loose. My body filled with a darkness that pulled me inward, downward, the party music growing faint, the bodies around me floating away until I was certain none of us actually existed.

I never told you that I saw you kissing her, that I watched you do it without hesitation, inching closer to her instead of backing away. I watched long enough to see her curl her fist under her chin to get more comfortable, the gesture natural and her proximity to you familiar, as if she had done it before. As if you both had done it before.

Still, I said nothing. I didn't want to be *that* woman, *that* wife. It was probably the party, I thought, the alcohol, I reasoned, that compelled you to do such a thing.

You were often senseless after drinking. Like the way you would insist on driving home after a night out, then cruise through yellow-lighted intersections faster than the speed limit allowed, all the while laying on the horn to let everyone know you were coming through, the windows down and the radio up as you laughed and hooted, hands light on the steering wheel.

MELISSA GRUNOW

Or how about when we were dating and you went out with your friends while I worked late, drove Kelly home, and kissed her before she could get out of the car? She pulled away and declared, "I'm not a homewrecker." You chased her up the walkway and toward the porch to talk about what had just happened and then you kissed her again, leaning into her, unable to stop, you said. You just couldn't stop.

The next day, you dragged me away from the front desk of the hotel where I worked and told me about it in the parking lot. I was in the middle of my shift folding Martex brand towels and watching daytime talk shows on mute when you arrived. You waited for me to say something. You waited, cried real tears, begged for forgiveness without concern.

You were drunk, you said. You had offered to drive her home, kissed her in the car once and then at the door because you were drunk, you said.

I nodded and felt nothing. I stared at the ground and exuded anger anyway.

Finally, I blamed her, and I forgave you.

You were drunk the first time we met, when Angie and I went to a party together at your house. I was under-age and showed up empty-handed, turning down all offers for drinks because I hadn't yet acquired the taste for beer. You danced with me in your living room, clinging to my hips as I shimmied to the music. You would apologize, back away, then grab my hips again. Your hands would slip around to the back pockets of my pants, sometimes squeezing, sometimes not, and I gave you that look that you would come to know, the one of discomfort and growing intolerance, but still I said nothing.

At your party, I had my eye on someone else, a graduate student like you, but one who was tall, pretty, and pretentious. I liked his quarter-zip sweater and dark jeans and was sitting next to him on the couch when you asked me to dance. I looked over to see if he saw your hands on my hips, but he was looking away, his attention elsewhere. Our eyes met briefly just before I turned around and found your inviting grin. At best, he found me immature. At worst, a tease, all because I allowed you to grab me repeatedly, and I didn't say anything or do anything to stop you.

I blamed the beer, and I forgave you.

We only fought once before we were married, but it was a fight that went on every day for an entire week, a fight that had no resolution without my absolute forgiveness. We had been dating a year and started planning a wedding even before you could afford a ring when you sat me down in my living room and told me you had a nine-year-old child in Minnesota that you hadn't seen in two years. It could no longer be both a secret and the truth.

"I love my son," you repeated, your face red and pinched and wet with tears when I spat accusations of neglect and indifference at you. "I love my son."

The lie bothered me because it felt like it should bother me. Everyone else was outraged, shocked, accusatory, dismissive. I accepted it with a heavy shrug, my eyes fixated on the dry and pudgy pink flesh of my always-cold hands. You had been trying to start over, to focus on your graduate program, to write without distractions of your past. And so, of your son, you said nothing.

I didn't want to watch you cry anymore, so I forgave you and welcomed him into my life.

In New Mexico, we shared a small one-bedroom apartment, checking account, car, some professors, and most of our friends. The first few months were spent living in a cave with heavy curtains of façade fabric that kept our fights secluded.

There was the time you came home drunk in the middle of the night and shook me awake with no purpose, mumbling questions about food, spinning accusations into poetics, punching me in the thigh when I begged to go back to sleep, and finally calling your brother to see advice of how to undo the already did. I disconnected the phone jack from the wall, fed up with your family's endless interference into our lives and the outrageous long-distance phone bills to Colorado. You picked up my coffee table and slammed it onto the floor, your jagged teeth snaring shouts that I couldn't hear because my gaze was fixated on the crack that inched its way up the sides and along the top of the lacquered wood, separating the table into two pieces, neither able to stand on just two legs.

After that first year, our marriage was a succession of practicalities, a collection of moments where we took turns shopping for cheaper car insurance, phone companies, apartments, moments where we felt like we had achieved some kind of milestone when we no longer had to share a car, upgraded to a two-bedroom place, got a second cat, secured full-time jobs. Our marriage was a checklist of achievements on display for others to realize and remind us that we had to be together for any of those things to happen. Our disagreements evolved from volatile to trivial, ones where I expressed disappointment over how much money you spent on specialty olive oil, and you complained that I gave my parents more gifts at Christmas time than you gave to yours. Shouts became eye rolls, and eventually slapping ceased altogether. Feigning happiness was the only thing we could agree on, but we both wondered when the day would come that I would roll over and face you one winter morning in the desert and say, "This is the end, isn't it?"

The *Flashdance* soundtrack ended and the stereo went quiet. I heard car doors slamming, tires kicking up gravel as partygoers drove away. The bedroom lights turned on, and Eliza stood over us to coax me and you out of her bed and into the one she set up for us on the futon in the living room. I opened my eyes slowly to find that everyone had left. Even Ginger was gone.

Did you ever write poems for her under the guise that they were for me? Was there something in the way she looked or smelled or sounded that compelled you to turn your face to her, your mouth to hers, to close your eyes and have a lover's moment with her instead of me? What would our lives be now, fifteen years later, if you hadn't kissed Ginger, if I had said something that night, the next day, or ever? Would you admit it if I asked you? Would you even remember that it happened?

I don't blame Ginger.

The light turned off on the other side of the bedroom door, and the house fell silent around us. A giant cockroach scurried out of the shadows and across the floor toward the futon. You looked alarmed until I stepped on it, its body cracked and oozed beneath my bare foot. In the morning, I threw up in the bathroom, alone and crippled on the floor as I heaved from too much vodka. You slept heavily and heedlessly on the futon, the blankets piled up high around you, unaware of my suffering. For that, I could never forgive you.

MELISSA GRUNOW

TOTALLY NORMAL UNTIL IT ISN'T

"What does all this mean finally, I kept asking like a college kid. Why does it make me want to cry? Maybe it's that we are all outsiders, we are all making our own unusual way through a wilderness of normality that is just a myth."

—ANNE RICE, *EXIT TO EDEN*

This is humiliating. I try to relax my shoulders and back against the table, with my heels in stirrups, my knees reluctantly moving apart, spreading my legs open.

I flinch as the ultrasound tech puts the gelled wand against my abdomen and searches for my empty uterus. "How long will this take?" I ask.

"If it goes in, less than five minutes." My doctor pulls on her gloves and sits down on a stool at the base of the exam table.

She doesn't answer the unasked question, "And what if it doesn't go in?" I tilt my chin upward and stare at the ceiling. There's not much else to look at.

My body is aching all over, but is most especially tender in my abdomen and lower back, since I'm just two days into my period. It's this unbearable pain that has brought me to this procedure in the first place. I take a few deep breaths and try to relax, but the discomfort stays. I try not to think about the menstrual blood that is inevitably leaking from my body that my gynecologist needs to navigate to guide the tube up my vagina and through the opening of my cervix to implant the IUD securely in my uterus.

Even in my thirties, lying on the table with my feet in stirrups is embarrassing, but to do so on my period is downright mortifying. However, the cervix is more relaxed during menstruation, which makes it easier and less painful to insert the IUD. That's the theory, anyway.

"I'll talk you through it," the doctor continues, and I notice she's not wearing a mask. How is she not just a little grossed out by the sight and the smell in front of her? Am I the only one in the room who wants to gag?

"Okay." I close my eyes for a moment and try to remind myself to breathe. Holding my breath will just make this experience even more unbearable, even though it seems to be my body's natural reaction.

"You ready?"

I nod a little and then realize she can't see me. "I think so." I close my eyes and imagine I'm in a yoga class contorting my body into eagle pose.

The top of her head bobs a little above the paper drape across my bent knees. "Your cervix is tilted to the right, which is totally normal, but it might make insertion a little difficult."

The words "totally normal" coming from a doctor never seem to mean actually normal. My cervix tilts to the right and my uterus tilts forward. My entire reproductive system is like a Tilt-a-Whirl, but this experience is no carnival ride.

"You're going to feel a little cramping."

It's as if I'm being impaled with a giant metal rod as the tube slides through my cervix and deposits the IUD into my uterus. I draw in my breath with a gasp and release it with a whimpering moan. I'm surprised to find that I'm crying. *How do women possibly handle having babies?*

MELISSA GRUNOW

"Here it is," the ultrasound tech says, pointing to the black and white screen next to her. "It's secure." I want to argue with her because the wand is closer to my left hip than squarely in the middle, but I can't think with a foreign object in my cervix.

The doctor says something, and then I feel her pull the tube out slowly. The speculum closes, and she's telling me to push back, that we're finished, that she'll see me again in a month to make sure everything is still in place.

"I left the strings a little long because they'll coil, and we don't want them to go up into the cervix. If they're bothering you or your partner, I can trim them a little when you come back." She picks up her laptop that's open to the screen with my medical history. "Any questions?"

"Not that I'm in the mood right now," I say, still crying, tears streaming down my temples and puddling in the grooves of my ears. "But when can I have sex again?"

She smiles a little. "Whenever you want. But if you want to wait a few days because you're not in the mood, you can use me as an excuse."

There is a pulsing pain burrowed into the center of my body. The ultrasound tech leaves the room so I can get dressed. I make the mistake of peeking under the discarded paper drape to find two thick smears of my blood soaked into the cover secured to the exam table.

The doctor had assured me that I would be fine, that maybe I would feel a little discomfort, but it was nothing that an over-the-counter painkiller couldn't fix. Yet, I move slowly through the waiting room and down the stairs, the aches pulsing throughout my entire core.

—

A child sits in front of me on an airplane, her mother next to her, and her father across the aisle. She drops her blanket on the floor without realizing, the plush fabric landing on the tired blue carpeting without a sound.

Passengers continue to push through to their seats, stepping on or over the blanket, each looking down at the obstruction, and promptly ignoring it.

I lean forward and pick it up. It's lime green and soft, a perfect travel blanket, especially for a five- or six-year-old, as this child appears to be. I reach over the arm of the girl's chair and dangle the blanket, trying to get her attention. Her father takes it from me and places it in her lap.

"Thank you," the girl says in a little voice.

I giggle at the sweetness and her gratitude. "You're welcome."

She again turns to smile at me. I can only see half of her face around the edge of the chair.

For a moment, I imagine she is mine and picture her climbing into my lap, pulling her soft blanket over us, and dozing together as the plane prepares for take-off.

Instead, she turns and faces forward, and all I see for the rest of the flight are the portions of her long, dark hair that fall behind her shoulder whenever she adjusts in her seat.

Months later while shopping for curtains, I find a blanket made from the same color and material. I open the package and run my hand along the inside, feeling the softness of the fabric. I don't need another blanket, but I buy it anyway.

⁓

My cycle is confused, and at nineteen, so am I. Three days on, four days off, a week on, a month off. It goes on like this for about six months before I tell my mom because I knew she would tell me to see a doctor, *her* doctor. I was dreading my feet in stirrups more than any kind of diagnosis, my body an embarrassment that was better kept hidden.

"He'll probably just put you on the pill," my mom said, as the pill is an easy answer to any woman's issue. "It will help regulate you."

After a brief physical exam and a round of blood work to test in a lab, I sit on the exam table fully clothed, swinging my legs back and forth, listening to the paper cover beneath me crinkle with each movement. I'm wishing I had brought the magazine from the waiting room. I'm wishing I had something to look at besides posters diagramming the fetal growth during a 40-week gestation. I'm wishing I wasn't so cold.

The doctor walks in while scanning my chart. He looks first at the lab numbers and then at my face. I always suspect that, without a chart, doctors have no idea who I am or why I'm there. I remember every detail, every spoken word from the previous visit. They remember nothing. To them, I am just another body in just another exam room.

He rolls his chair over to me and shows me numbers in various columns, explaining the range for each.

Normal. Normal. Normal. Normal. *Elevated.*

"It's a slight variance, but still beyond the normal range." He moves the tip of his pen from one column to the next as if I can't see the correlation for myself. "What this tells me is that you have something called Polycystic Ovarian Syndrome."

I only recognize the words "ovarian" and "syndrome," without any real understanding of what a syndrome is. "Is that a disease?" I ask.

"It's a condition." He scribbles a prescription on a pad. "I'm going to start you on oral contraceptives." He hands me the piece of paper.

"But what does it *mean*?" I don't have the words I need to ask the right questions. I can't do anything but stare at him and try to read his body language.

He writes something again and rips the page from the top of the pad. "Here," he says. "You can research it."

I look down and see the diagnosis in dark blue block letters: Polycystic Ovarian Syndrome. PCOS.

The doctor is gone before I have the chance to think of another question, the door quietly clicking shut behind him.

～

I'm sitting on the carpet, banging a toy drum stick against a toy drum and belting out the Alphabet Song at the top of my lungs while Ryan squeals in delight. Even Jaren—who is a few years older and sensitive to noise—joins the band by picking up a plastic trumpet and blowing into it full force.

The other adults are in the kitchen, hovering around the refrigerator and sipping beverages, as Nancy moves from counter to sink to stove to counter, lining up the many dishes of Thanksgiving dinner in a buffet line.

A few of them peek into the living room, and I overhear someone telling my boyfriend how good I am with kids, how I'll make a great mother someday.

"She's so patient," his aunt tells him. "The boys just love her!"

I bang the drum harder and move on to "Old McDonald Had a Farm," getting Ryan and Jaren to join in at the *E-I-E-I-O* until our voices overcome the kitchen chatter.

～

I move my fingers across the keyboard, and hundreds of thousands of websites and discussion forums generate when I hit the search button. I click on various links, skim, move to another.

I don't know what I'm looking to find. Causes? Description? Implications? What is this supposed to mean for me? I jot down symptoms as I find them, and check off the ones that apply.

MELISSA GRUNOW

✓ Acne

✓ Difficulty maintaining or losing weight

✓ Extra body hair (chin, chest, belly)

✓ Thinning hair

✓ Irregular periods

✓ Depression

I keep reading. So far, nothing I can't live with, nothing that I haven't already gotten used to living with.

Then, the grand finale: infertility.

I sit back in my chair and stare at the words. *Women with PCOS may have difficulty getting pregnant* and *PCOS makes it difficult to conceive.*

One website describes a defective pituitary gland center in which fertility begins to resemble a man's (constant), rather than a woman's (cyclical). That hormone imbalance prevents ovulation, which affects the likelihood of conception. Birth control pills are used to balance these hormones, but one very intentional side effect to contraception is the inability to get pregnant. That's where the cycle fails. I decide to stop taking the pill, as it seems unnecessary to fake a hormone balance.

There is the assumption that when a woman reaches adulthood she will—at some point—have a child, maybe even a few children. There is also the assumption that within all of us lays an inherent desire to have children, that the proverbial clock begins to tick because our bodies were designed to breed.

My fertility clock doesn't sound on the hour anymore.

—

I stand in the parking lot talking to Heather after our yoga class, our rolled mats snug in carrying cases slung over our shoulders.

"Avery's colic isn't as bad anymore," she says. I'm pulled from distant thoughts and realize we are—again—talking about her baby.

"That must be so hard." I don't know what else to say.

She nods. She's grateful she has maternity leave from teaching kindergarten at a special school for deaf/hard of hearing children. "We're lucky," she says.

I had made the requisite visit to their house to meet the baby a few weeks prior before our class. Heather's daughter, like her, is small and blonde. When I pulled her into my cradled arms, she had squirmed and fussed. Finally, she settled into sleep, as I tickled her lower back with the hand propped under her body. I immediately loved her.

Heather had sat across from us and smiled a new mother's smile, though she admitted that she felt her once-slender body had betrayed her and the lack of sleep was making her impatient and often angry. I had coaxed her to come to yoga with me every week, and Steve had agreed to stay with Avery.

I had also invited her to come to class with me in an effort to maintain our friendship. She would not be the first, or the fifth, or even the tenth friend that I've lost to motherhood.

Heather shifts her mat to the other shoulder. "It's such an incredible thing, being a mom."

I smile. I've heard this before. Motherhood is such an ordinary concept in general, but an extraordinary experience for the woman. Every friend of mine who becomes a mother acts as though no one else has ever done it before, that it makes her some kind of superhero.

"I think back to who I was before Avery," she continues. "I was just so *selfish*. Everything was about *me*. Nothing is about me anymore."

I do my best to keep my posture, but the statement cuts through every part of me. *I am not selfish*, I want to say, but the words don't matter. Instead, I lean in to hug her good-bye and tell her I'll see her at class next week.

I haven't seen her since.

—

I'm in a pool hall in a small town in New Mexico, snacking on pizza and sipping a watery draft beer. There is music reminiscent of high school blasting from the jukebox, and most of my friends are taking advantage of free pool night, playing game after game, and dropping plastic shot glasses into plastic cups to make Irish Car Bombs.

I'm seated at the bar listening to Bethany tell the story of how she ended up in New Mexico after growing up in Florida. Stories of a failed relationship with a man who sold her belongings to repay money she lent him, and others of growing up in foster care then trying as an adult to establish a bond with her estranged father.

The bartender brings us a round of drinks and points to the dusty construction workers a few stools away. "These are on them."

Bethany leans in and smiles. "You must be ovulating," she says, as if it's my fertility that has radiated throughout the room and coerced the others to spend their hard-earned money on us.

I smile softly at her joke, and together we raise our glasses to the generous men, but we leave our interactions at that.

My body continues to empty my womb on the third week of every month. There is no risk when there is nothing at stake. It's the wash cycle and then the rinse cycle.

—

I'm in a basement bar in Petoskey, seated across from a man I've known for less than a month, and yet here we are on vacation together in a romantic northern Michigan town. It's our last night out before our drive home in the morning, and the conversations now include visions of the future.

It's the conversation I never want to have, yet it's the conversation that I always need to have.

"Do you want kids?" His question is gentle. *He* is gentle.

I lift the pint glass to my lips and take a long drink before I answer. "No."

His face relaxes. It's the most pensive I've seen him since we met. "No?"

I shake my head, my eyes looking at anything but his. "I can't."

He looks uncomfortable, and I feel obligated to elaborate.

"I have this condition," I say. "It will be difficult to conceive. I've known for fourteen years, so I've just kind of accepted it. I don't really have the desire, anyway. I understand why people have kids, but I don't see a place for them in my life."

He's quiet. This isn't what men like to hear, even men who themselves aren't ready to start a family. Every man I've ever known imagines himself as a father someday.

"Men have left me because of this before," I say. "I'll understand if it's something you can't live with. It's something you would have to give up to be with me. I won't change my mind." I press my fingertip to the base of my eye to prevent tears from smearing my makeup.

Chris takes my hand. "I like you," he says and his lips curl upward in the way that they do when he is being genuine. "I want to see where this goes."

I nod and force a tired smile. It won't be the last time we have this conversation.

~

Another doctor. Another prognosis. This time my periods have become so heavy and so painful that I'm either missing a day of work each month or giving lectures while seated at the front of the room to prevent myself from fainting in front of my students.

I have an expensive ultrasound to screen for polyps, and everything is normal. I have bloodwork done, and it comes back normal. I alter my diet and get more exercise, but nothing changes. It's all normal, normal, normal.

I go in for a consult to discuss my options. I refuse the pill. The other two choices are procedural: uterine ablation, which is to cauterize the uterus lining with a laser. The other is implantation of an intrauterine device that would stay in for five years. Both prevent pregnancy. With the first option, though, pregnancy prevention is certain, and the rare change of pregnancy could cause death.

It takes me months to make the decision. Publicly, everyone who knows me knows I don't want children. Privately though, I can't help but listen, at least a little, to the persuasive voices of others who insist that someday I'll change my mind because it's unnatural to not want them. The idea of scarring the lining of my uterus is too absolute for comfort. An IUD would give me some relief and a little more time to make any kind of permanent decision.

The week before my IUD procedure, I ask Chris to drive me to my appointment. "They tell me it's not a big deal. It only takes a few minutes, I guess, and I'll be okay to drive. I'm just not so sure that I'll *want* to drive."

"Yeah, I can do that." I can see the introspection move across his face like a shadow. "What's the procedure?"

It's easier to have awkward, medically technical conversations in the shower when you're both naked and vulnerable and neither one of you can just walk away. I choose the moment when I have my eyes closed while washing my hair as the moment to explain it to him. He listens but doesn't respond.

After the procedure, I meet Chris in the waiting room and barely make eye contact as I motion to him to follow me out the door. I take the stairs without thinking, and wince with each step, with one hand cradling my lower back and the other resting on my abdomen. He doesn't ask if I'm okay. He can tell that I am not.

When I get home, Chris prepares a heating pad for my stomach and rubs my back until I fall asleep, the caregiver in him natural and benevolent. When I wake from short naps, he brings me water and painkillers, and hugs me when I cry from the unrelenting pain. I am cradled and comforted.

⁓

At my aunt's surprise sixtieth birthday party, children untie helium balloons from centerpieces and chase each other around the room with them. Eventually the strings come loose, and the balloons float to the ceiling. The kids climb up onto chairs and jump as high as they can, but it's still not high enough to reclaim their balloons.

Chris and I stand near the buffet table as my cousin talks incessantly about her all-natural herbal weight-loss enterprise, which sounds more like a pyramid scheme to me than a successful business. I listen to her pitch and vacantly nod, while Chris is politely attentive. My niece Madison marches up to him, her elaborate dress rustling with each step, and points up to the balloon that has floated up to the ceiling above our heads.

He stretches upward and brings it down for her, a giant red one that she clutches with both hands. She runs off to play again until someone else lets go of their balloon, and the process repeats itself.

I watch him as he moves around the room to follow another child's runaway balloon, responding patiently and thoughtfully to each request, smiling each time a new child

MELISSA GRUNOW

shyly approaches him. He's comfortable in this role, more comfortable than making small talk with my distant relatives, yet he's not fussy and overbearing. For the next hour, he lets the children come to him and offers assistance when he notices the younger ones that are about to cry when their balloons escape. I feel a pull in my gut that I don't recognize. I know in that moment that I want a future with this man, and perhaps it's a future that I have not yet been able to imagine.

CAN I KEEP YOU?

"If you gaze long into an abyss, the abyss will gaze back into you."
—FRIEDRICH NIETZSCHE

He had been speaking for ten minutes about a girl named Maureen, who he also referred to as Mo, also referred to as "my girlfriend." She was a residence life director in Indiana, he said, and he continued on about something to do with long-distance relationships, how they met, and something else that I couldn't hear over the voice of dissent in my head. *But he's gay,* I thought. *He's got to be gay. Isn't he?*

"So," I started, dragging the word into multiple syllables to give me time to put my thoughts together before he went on with another story that would fill me with more questions. He had been on the job for a week, and aside from a telephone interview, an internet screening, and a brief orientation, I knew very little about him. "Who is Ian?"

He let out a loud cackle, his boxy beaver teeth revealed between smiling lips. The laugh broke the din of the neon-lighted restaurant, and patrons at a nearby table looked curiously in our direction. He stirred his frozen margarita and ignored the onlookers, even though he watched as my eyes looked around to see who was staring. He seemed amused by my discomfort, and it intrigued me.

"I mean, your Facebook profile says you're in a relationship with someone named Ian. He's obviously not the girlfriend you just mentioned," I continued.

He laughed his shrieking hyena laugh again as if to say, *gotcha!* "You shouldn't believe everything you read on Facebook." His eyes settled on mine until I had to look away, my cheeks burning from what I thought to be the tequila or maybe the humid August evening. I sipped down swallows of ice water to cool my body from the inside out.

—

I knocked on his open door and stepped inside his office. "Can you go to the celebration dinner after training on Friday? Or are you leaving for Indiana right after your presentation?"

We were supposed to have meetings once a week, but he invented reasons to come into my office at least once a day. The office visits increased, and soon I found myself wandering into his, just barely lingering in the doorway as if I had somewhere better to be, but what I had to say couldn't wait and didn't have the patience for email. We always talked about work, about program planning, about making the greatest impact for the students. They were leaders in the making, and it was our job to create opportunities for them to lead the way. The success of our programming was essential to his longevity, since his position was grant-funded and predicated on outcomes assessment. If we worked hard enough, planned long enough, and interacted more than enough, I would be able to keep his position, and maybe even him, long-term.

"Mo broke up with me," he said. "So I'll be there."

"Oh." I couldn't say that I was sorry. He always spoke of her in past-tense as if she was already gone. I invited him to have a beer with me after work so he wouldn't be alone.

"I think I'm just going to go home." He didn't add "and cry," but my memory adds it for him.

Later that night he sent me a text. "Let's go out on Friday. Somewhere close to your house. I'll probably need to crash on your couch after."

—

He turned his face toward mine and moved his body in. I angled my neck, tilted my head back, away, my mouth upward. He moved in again. I lingered there, waiting. His arm was tight around my back, taunting me with the proximity of his lips, and then he moved in all the way, his mouth on mine, breathing heavy breath, and we kissed on the couch in my basement because he wasn't sober enough to drive home, because his girlfriend had broken up with him, because there was nothing stopping us. We kissed, we groped, we breathed in each other's pain and misery and hurt and disregard and we sighed through it, moaned through it, kept our mouths busy through it so neither of us could speak up, say stop, say we shouldn't be doing this, say this is wrong.

—

"I want to look like Kesha," he told the Chinese woman while she fitted him with a wig cap, and he stared at his reflection in the mirror.

She didn't flinch, as if men frequently wandered into her store with their not-girlfriends and requested to look like pop singers. "I don't know that," she said.

He searched for images on his phone and showed her one of a superstar with mascara artfully smeared below her eyes. The Chinese woman nodded, clapped a little, and walked off to find the perfect wig.

It was two weeks before Halloween, but he wasn't buying it for Halloween.

In drag, he called himself Alice, and he was going to introduce her to me for the first time. He lived in a wonderland of performativity. It was a world I didn't understand. He was gentle but unrelenting, though, as he took my hand and led me down the rabbit hole. I shielded my face as we descended together, terrified that I couldn't see the bottom, had no idea how to predict the end. He was a man who was a woman who was a man, a clashing of binaries that caused a hiccup in my step as I carefully tiptoed around the question of who was he *really*?

But he didn't let me tumble. He didn't let me to fall.

All I knew was that at night, in the dark, he was all man, all mine, and he could keep me as long as he would have me. I clung to that, idealized the fantasy of him, of me, of us. It would be the single most important act of defiance against normativity that I could conjure. What if we survived it? I wondered. What if we survived each other?

⁓

The breeze coming in through the open window chilled me awake. The temperature had dropped considerably that week as it often did when the warm weather lingered shyly at the onset of autumn. Nightfall was heavy in the room and only moonlight filtered in through the cracked blinds.

In the dark, my voice was a scratch of a whisper. "Can I keep you?" I pressed my chilled fingertips into his back and felt his heat run through them.

His breath slowed to a sigh, and he turned toward me, nuzzling his forehead against my cheek. It was the only way he could look at me and away from me at the same time. I felt his body relax against mine as he fell back asleep. An answer left unspoken was better than a reassuring lie, and so much better than the truth. In the meantime, anyway. I could hang on for the meantime.

We went to every campus event together and had our picture taken at all of them. We would throw our arms around each other and smile as if to say, "Look! We're great friends! Look! We're an unstoppable team! Look! There's more going on here, and you would see it if you would just look! *Look.*"

Photos were posted and tagged on Facebook, and we lived in each other's social media as much as we did each other's offices, text messages, and lives. On the nights we were apart, we fell asleep on the phone together like we were in high school. At my house, he took over a dresser drawer and filled it with warm socks and hooded sweatshirts. He put leftovers in my fridge and reheated them in the toaster oven. His apartment remained vacant most of the time and completely absent of me. Of the few times I had been there, I didn't leave anything behind. In his world, I didn't exist.

I waited for someone to say something, to ask, "What's going on with you two?"

And yet, nobody noticed.

Whenever he shrieked his ostentatious laugh, I never understood why no one saw the person sitting next to him, the person accompanying the loudest person in the room. To me it seemed our entire relationship was a storefront window, a fishbowl, a voyeur's playground. What I didn't consider, though, was that maybe everyone else assumed he was gay like I had before I got to know him. With his slender physique and high-pitched laugh, his gentle lisp voice, and his activism in the LGBT community, he masqueraded as the assumed. Yet, I saw him through every mask, every fanfare, every feather, all the makeup, and he could do nothing but return my gaze.

We met up at a bar on a Saturday afternoon, sat together on the patio, and ordered a beer. I yanked the zipper on my hoodie as high as it would go. It was probably the last weekend of the season that we would be able to sit outside. Winter was upon us.

We made small talk. We nibbled on mozzarella sticks. I almost choked on my beer when he asked me, "Where do you see this going?"

I pinched my face in dread and ordered another drink. "I don't know."

"Because I've been thinking about it."

"Oh?"

He crossed his legs tightly together like a woman, in a way thick thighs like mine wouldn't allow for me to imitate. "I don't feel anything for you. I've tried. I've thought about it. But there's nothing there." He gestured with his hands, but stared down at the table as he spoke. It was humiliating.

I felt that familiar weight in my gut, the sting of self-doubt, the hollowed response of deception. I refused to look at him. He couldn't have my gaze. Not there, not then.

"I know you don't want to hear this," he continued. "But it's because of your size. And because you're my boss and we want different things. But mostly because of your size."

I put down the mozzarella stick and spit what I was chewing into a napkin. "I'll stop eating." I was a little taller than he was and a healthy weight for my height. But next to him, I was a giant.

"Don't do that."

"You don't get to say that to me."

"It won't change anything. There's no future here."

I felt my body funnel into itself and gather into a puddle on the concrete. We were the embodiment of semantic dissidence living in a linguistic black hole. Our relationship was a test of the system, an experiment of authority. It was set up to fail because it wasn't anything of substance. After the bill was paid, we left separately and agreed to only interact in our shared professional setting.

We lasted just one week apart.

⌒

We drove eight hours together to Washington, D.C., so that I could be elected president of a board of directors for a non-profit that I didn't know how to run. I was nominated and voted in at the start of the meeting while I sat at someone else's dining table and blushed, ate another chocolate chip cookie from the generic grocery store container, and allowed board members to congratulate me for something I didn't want to win. In three weeks, I would resign, having done nothing to perpetuate our mission. I was in no position to give guidance to anyone on anything.

He got so drunk our first night in Virginia that he didn't remember anything that happened after we left the bar. He paid his tab, slid his credit card back into his wallet, walked out the front door, and stepped into darkness.

But I remember. I remember him reaching for me in the night, tugging on my clothes, then his, and not because he wanted me, not because he wanted it. No, it was to try and sober up, to make the room stop spinning.

The next day, we took pictures in front of national monuments. At the end of the day, we settled in at a restaurant that he chose—one that was overpriced and didn't have enough food and served peas (*peas!*) in the pasta sauce. I was hungry, and that hunger found a solid space of empty inside me. Maybe the space and the walking and the climbing and the laughing and the wondering what he was thinking would help my stomach flatten out. Maybe we would drive back to Michigan and realize the trip had bonded us, and that maybe his declarations that I wasn't attractive because I was bigger than him, maybe all of those things would fix themselves with a road trip to the nation's capital, a weekend's worth of nights at the Red Roof Inn, accidentally discovering a local cover band at a bar called Sweet Caroline's, eating in restaurants that didn't give us enough food, and taking turns smiling for a camera that couldn't capture our expressions because our eyes hid behind dark sunglasses. Maybe, after all that, I could keep him. Maybe he would decide to keep me.

No. The trip was the beginning of the end. The end of our friendship. The end of our affair. The end of his job less than two months later when I fired him for sleeping with a student employee.

Fraternization was grounds for termination because his position was government-regulated, and she was a tuition-paying customer. It should have applied to me, but it didn't. That was the loophole. What I had done was wrong. But what *he* did, *that* was against the rules.

The girl had actively pursued him since the night he got drunk at a student event and danced with her for hours while I sipped water from the sidelines feeling like a chaperone until I had to carry him to the car and lecture him about what getting involved with a student could do to him, what it was doing to me. He sat in the passenger seat, hands in his lap, head down, face blank, and nodded, assuring me he knew better, assuring me it wouldn't happen again. Then it happened again.

He was an hour late for work the day I fired him. He was often late for work, but so was I. Nobody was watching me, though, and so he thought nobody was watching him.

I was. I had been, anyway. When he arrived, I called him onto my office, told him to pack his things, and gave him twenty-four hours to vacate his campus apartment.

I had his full attention. "Okay," he croaked. "But why?"

I slid the report across the table and pointed to the infraction, the pictures that had been posted on Facebook of them dancing together, the timestamped security footage of her going in and out of his apartment, the way she had replaced me so quickly that my face felt as though it were sucking on lemons.

He nodded a single nod. He pursed his lips in defeat, tapped his knuckles on the tabletop once, stood up, and was gone.

I didn't monitor him to make sure he didn't steal anything as he packed his belongings. I didn't call security to escort him off campus. I didn't draw any more attention to my blatant retaliation than I had to.

Silence fell over our office. There was no laughter. There was nothing but the standard awkward tension that follows a termination.

I left work early and hunched over my kitchen table where I had sat with him so many times before, each of us staring into laptops and working together on yet another program. The silence clawed at me like a dark shadow ready to sink its nails into my duplicitous soul. I turned the ringer on my cell phone up as high as it would go in anticipation of the call that would end my career. I practiced my justifications, speaking to an empty room. "He crossed the line by sleeping with a student." "He had been warned." "He's done this before, he told me so." *He's done this before.* "It's my duty to protect our students."

I fixated on the wall in front of me and practiced my truth over and over while I waited. An hour went by. Then another. I checked my email. Nothing. No demands for explanations. No messages from my supervisor requesting a meeting. Nothing from the funding agency asking for a response to any accusations against me. He had gone away quietly, his position cut short and his career threatened, and I could go on as if I had never even known him.

MELISSA GRUNOW

He never called me out on my hypocrisy. *He didn't let me tumble; he didn't let me fall.*

After finding his deodorant in my bathroom and pajama bottoms in my drawer, I drank a bottle of wine on an empty stomach, then threw up into my kitchen sink. I sent him a text asking him when he would get his things. I received no answer.

He deleted his Facebook account that day, and with it, all of our photos together, all of our shared experiences that should have left everyone wondering, but that no one said anything about—not then, not ever.

The girl's profile stayed active, and for a week she had one lone status update: "Strength will find you sooner than you thought it could." Before that, months prior, she responded to a post he was tagged in. "I love his laugh!" she had written. Otherwise, there was no public evidence that they were anything more than acquaintances.

You shouldn't believe everything you read on Facebook.

Was it my motive to protect her, though? If not her, then who? I was beyond saving. So was he. So was the program he was developing that died with his termination.

I considered emailing the student and requesting a meeting with her to explain that it wasn't her fault, that it would be the right thing to put her emotional well-being before my own. All that would do, though, was make me out to be some kind of hero, and I wasn't. Neither was she. There were no victims. There were only perpetrators.

I fell asleep early, and woke up early, the sky still dark outside my window. As daylight devoured the few remaining stars not already hidden by urban smog, I pulled away the covers and rose to my feet in a room that had cooled with the onset of winter. I had met him in August. By December, he had vanished. For just one season, I had kept him. For just one season, he had let me.

BEFORE AND AFTER

"Everything around me is evaporating. My whole life, my memories, my imagination and its contents, my personality—it's all evaporating. I continuously feel that I was someone else, that I felt something else, that I thought something else."
—FERNANDO PESSOA, *THE BOOK OF DISQUIET*

There was the before and now there is the after.
Every threat in my waking life haunts me in my
dreams. You linger deep in my subconscious
and when I finally try to rest my mind at night,
you come out to play, to taunt, to beckon from
the fringes of a broken place within me. I can
handle it when you appear as a single father
with three young children in your car, pound on
my door, and insist I give you a place to sleep
for the night, even though this cabin is a rental
and nobody is allowed to sleep here but me.
You pound until the glass breaks, and I wander
around the cabin unplugging every electronic
from every outlet because I can't get the volume
under control, and it is so loud, so loud.

I can handle when you manifest as the man I
trust the most who says he's moving back to

MELISSA GRUNOW

Michigan and into a large house with low ceilings that would require crawling about a bedroom that I would make my own, but do I want to sell my home and move in anyway? *Yes*, I will respond. *Yes, yes, of course*, as the you who isn't you asserts, *I love you. I've always loved you.*

Sometimes the world is on fire. Sometimes the world is under water. Sometimes you appear just to push me deeper. Sometimes you appear to pull me to the surface just as I am about to relinquish breath. Sometimes my skin blisters, my hair singes away. Sometimes I gasp and awaken. Sometimes I know I am dreaming and beg to wake up but you laugh, laugh, laugh, and say, *You asked for this. You know you did.*

I can't handle it when you show up in the form of my dog who is a golden retriever in my dreams instead of a husky, but I recognize him anyway. He lies down at me feet, takes a deep breath, and dies. *What do I do with your body?* I ask before I wake up thirty minutes before my alarm wondering who is crying and how to quiet the noise until I realize it is me, it is me.

⁓

In the before, everything is hopeful. In the after, everything is ephemeral.

⁓

Tell me you love me, you said. I lied. I lied and said what you wanted to hear. Lying is so easy when I whisper into the darkness. I make promises that I don't intend to keep. *Give me a year*, you insisted, even though the vodka tonic you paid for only lasted that night. *Why a year?* I asked. It was such a long time. Too many days, too many seasons. *Because that's what I need.* I should have known then your needs were too demanding, rigid, unrelenting, selective, precise.

⁓

To you, I was a vessel, a portal to another unimaginable dimension. Too bad I talked too much. Too bad I asked too many questions. Too bad I insisted on veracity. Too bad, indeed.

⁓

When you slapped my dog on the nose, the look in his eyes as he winced and backed away broke my heart. He had never been slapped before. He had never been anything but loved.

Please don't hit my dog. Tell him no,
and he will leave you alone.

I told him no! Are you fucking deaf? Not
everyone is going to love your dog.

The thing is though, everyone does.

Strangers at the campground, kids, neighbors, people driving by while we're out for a walk, all telling me he's beautiful or they ask questions or they stop to pet him and comment on his gentle demeanor and all-around good behavior.

MELISSA GRUNOW

*Not everyone is going to love your
dog,* you said again.

I nodded, knowing it wasn't true but
tired of arguing. I wanted to say, *You
mean not everyone is going to love you.*

⌣

There is a place where men do not hit
or yell because in that place, men do
not exist. I have yet to find it.

⌣

I died the day you killed me. I die every day
knowing you have gone on living the life you want
to live. The change is imprinted on my DNA,
a somatic mutation of the self that cannot be
passed on to another. The gene pool stops here.

⌣

I could tolerate that you held my glassware to the
light and complained of dust and fingerprints, even
when it was still warm from the dishwasher. I could
tolerate that you wouldn't accept water from the
tap or ice from my freezer because you didn't trust
that it was safe, that you didn't trust municipalities
that have lied to residents before about the lead
content of their water. I could tolerate that you had
a wife you loved and would not leave, no steady
job to speak of, a past full of secrets and ambiguous
timelines. I could tolerate that you changed
your name to denounce your father, became the
noun—the label—of what you desired to be. It
was a portrayal of a self that others recognized and
accepted. That was who you were, and so it was.

I could tolerate your assertiveness and
passionate exhalations that appeared very
much like aggression because they made my
large self feel small, and I longed to be an
object of affection, a tiny woman, a *petit moi.*

I could tolerate it all because when you
smiled it seemed genuine and when you
fucked me you whispered, *I need you.*

~

Get on your knees.

Please don't humiliate me.

Get, you said as you shoved me
downward, *on your knees.*

My body fell to the floor like crumpled paper,
waifish and defeated. You unzipped your
jeans, grabbed my head with both hands,
and forced my voice from my throat.

~

Someone once told me that there are fewer
crimes committed on dead end streets because
criminals don't want to limit themselves
to one exit. Safety in one's home increases
as opportunities to escape decrease.

There is one way in, one way out, unless you
know about the unpaved semi-secluded alley
rampant with potholes large enough to swallow
boulders. Theoretically, you can exit that way,

MELISSA GRUNOW

but only if you didn't pop a tire or break an axle
or bottom out, scraping the undercarriage as
the shocks and struts grow weaker with each
rise and fall while speeding through the alley,
kicking up mud and debris, tires spinning and
sliding, grip tight on the steering wheel.

*Don't leave candles burning. Don't walk away
from a pot boiling on the stove. Always close the
garage door. Keep the barricade on the fence so it
can't be opened from the outside. Don't answer the
door unless you're expecting someone. Draw the
curtains and blinds at night to block the view from
the sidewalk. Don't leave your car unlocked. Don't
leave the windows open, not even a crack. Carry
pepper spray when you walk the dog at night.*

The home is a sanctuary. All you have to
do is follow basic safety rules. That was the
before, however. The after is quite different.

I wanted a home place that was of my own
making, followed my own rules, and met my
own needs for safety. I thought I had found it.

—

You have everything a man could want,
you said. *You have everything a man
could want, but you need to be loved.*

I am insufficient, an object of a
taken man's insatiable desire.

I could feel your eyes on me as I read from an essay about volunteering in Haiti. It was hard to ignore you, the only black man in a room of white faces while I extolled on the social and economic implications of skin tone in a country where villages are at the mercy of unmerciful storms and a corrupt government. I became acutely aware of my privilege to give voice to something I perhaps could never understand.

When you invited me out for a drink afterward, I hesitated, though I didn't flinch. I felt a tug at the base of my skull to decline, but I shrugged an acceptance anyway. You were disarming and it unnerved me.

That is the moment I wish I could return to, the moment where everything I had come to understand about my world unraveled.

Regret, they tell me, is simply a replacement for blame.

You don't need a man to tell you the things that are self-apparent, you said. *You're better than that.*

And yet—

⁓

At the bar, I had a nearly full drink in front of me and was in the middle of telling a story when you spoke over me. *I'm fifty-one,* you said. *I'm*

MELISSA GRUNOW

married. Your admittance was straightforward
and unemotional, the lights reflecting off your
glasses. You leaned on the bar with your elbow
and angled your body toward me, annoyed that
other patrons kept bumping the back of your
chair. *Do you want to go for a walk?* you asked.

When I tried to participate in the conversation,
you guffawed at the sound of my voice
and said you forgave me for interrupting
you, even though I hadn't apologized.

I wanted to leave. I should have
left then, but I didn't.

Instead, I let you kiss me on the street, your
hands gripping the back of my head.

⌣

You recognized in me all the love I had to give,
the swallowing nature of my heart, the generosity
of self from guilt. I want being in love to feel like
wind in my hair, free-falling from the sky, yet
knowing I won't crash to the ground, trusting
there is always a parachute and a safety net. There
is always someone to catch me when I don't even
know I'm falling. That, though, was before.

⌣

There was no love between us. There were
your pedantic expectations, rather than
authenticity. Everything was about what it
appeared to be. It was as though I were some
kind of investment, a seed project, and you

a budding entrepreneur that was sure this
time, with me, was worth the gamble.

I hadn't loved you when I died. I didn't even
really like you that much anymore. The
truth is, I don't know anyone who does.

⌣

You said you liked the way I wore my hair, so I cut it.
You said you've always had a thing for redheads, so I
dyed it dark purple, almost black. You said you liked
the shape of my body, so I hid it beneath baggy
clothes as the weight that gave me curves fell away.

You told the detective you wouldn't speak to
him without a lawyer, so he closed the case
without having all of the evidence, the rape kit
sitting in a locker somewhere, unprocessed.

To deny is to excuse. We are all cowards
in our own way. I remain hidden behind
drawn curtains. You remain protected
by bureaucracy. That is the after.

⌣

I shudder when the phone rings because it might
be you calling. I live with the curtains drawn,
the lights off, stiffening each time a car drives
down the street playing loud music for fear it
might be you about to pull into the driveway.

You told me to be wary of my neighbor who
sits on his front porch smoking cigarettes as he
watches you come and go. *He's harmless*, I said.

Are you fucking him?

Of course not. I don't even know his name.

The real monster is you, the man sitting on
the edge of my bed while I cower under the
covers and bleed you onto my sheets.

⁓

I dreamt of you last night. Even in the
dream, I was surprised it was you.

The rain scratching at the windows filled me
with the same dread as if it were an animal
clawing its way through to pounce, to attack.

The thunder pulled me from my dream.
I was startled and woke with shaky
nerves, and the unsettled mind that can
only occur when being ripped from one
state of consciousness into another.

There is grief in the aftermath. The logistics of
day-to-day life require attention, even when our
minds and bodies are not able to keep moving.

I have spent more time mourning you
than I ever spent knowing you. How
do I allow myself to breathe? How do I
allow myself the space to just be?

Nothing in your life has changed.
Everything has changed for me.

*Sometimes when women say stop, they don't
mean it*, you said when I finally confronted
you. *It was just a misunderstanding.*

⁓

For two hours, I cried. For four hours
I slept fitfully in the same bed, on the
same sheets, my body still naked, bruises
forming on my hips, broken.

For two days, I stayed home from work because I
couldn't sit in a chair. I ignored your phone calls,
your text messages, willing away your existence.

I grieved the loss of myself. No, it's in
present tense. I grieve, perpetually.

⁓

You pin the back of my legs down with
your knees, my hips with your hands, and
I can't move, can't get away and run.

The pain shoots up my spine in screams that
fill the enclosing space around my head. I
don't recognize myself in those screams, not
even when my own voice begs, *Stop it! Stop it!
Stop it!* in shrieking bursts. I try to army crawl
away until I'm pinned face-down between
my headboard and the weight of your body.
Shhhhh, you say between moans. *Shhhhh.*

My world stops. The music stops. Eventually
my screaming stops, and I succumb to

MELISSA GRUNOW

the end of my life. Sirens ring in my head.
I might faint. I might throw up.

You collapse briefly against me, and my skin
catches fire underneath you. I turn my head
and meet your gaze, your face bearing an
expression that burns into my memory. You run
your hand down the length of my back, pat my
thigh twice and say, *You needed to be raped.*

I want to die, and so I do. It's two kinds
of *la petite mort*, but I am the one who
cannot be revived. That is the after.

⌣

When did you break up?

I stammered through a summation
of the preceding three weeks.

The judge's clerk looked bored with
me. *But when did you break up?*

I didn't have a definitive answer because there
had not been a relationship. *I pressed charges
against him. Isn't that a clear enough message?*

No, he said. *No,* said the judge when she scrawled,
"Insufficient allegations" on the bottom of
the form next to the checkbox that read, "The
petition for an ex parte personal protection
order is dismissed without notice of the right

to request a hearing because the petitioner's
claims are sufficiently without merit."

—

*This is Detective P——. The prosecutor's office
denied issuing a warrant for arrest at this time.*

—

In my living room, you sat on my couch and
strummed your guitar, coaxing me to drink more.
That was the before, though. That was before.

—

I wake up and expel the contents of my
stomach into the toilet. The text message
from you reads, *That was… great.*

—

There is denial in the after. *I've been falsely
accused of sexual assault,* you said into a
microphone, blinking and smirking at the
camera on your computer. *It didn't happen. And
that had to go to the police department and that
had to go to discussion and it was humiliating.
It was to me personally humiliating, and it isn't
something I would wish upon anyone. What
do you do for that person who is not guilty?*

I seethed as I watched you declare your
innocence and broadcast it on the Internet.

I have pictures and video of consensual—

You looked away from the microphone and
chuckled. You couldn't even bring yourself
to say what it was. *I have pictures and video.*

MELISSA GRUNOW

In the before, I didn't know I was being
photographed and filmed. In the after,
your digital recordings of corroboration
only assure me of one fact: it was not
only intentional; it was premeditated.

⏤

You may assert the other side of a two-sided
story, but I am the warden of truth. You are
forever the shadow in my periphery, the stain
on my carpet, the bruise on my back. There is
only the after, and in the after, there is nothing
for you to claim. This is my narrative now.

PART 2
DISPLACED

INTENTIONS

"Our greatest pretenses are built up not to hide the evil and the ugly in us, but our emptiness. The hardest thing to hide is something that is not there."
—ERIC HOFFER, *THE PASSIONATE STATE OF MIND*

You approached me on the street, in the dark. "Do you have a light?" you asked. The tall buildings on either side of us created shadows on your face. On your head, you wore a hat. On your shoulder, you wore a bag.

In your hands, you held nothing, most notably, not a cigarette.

With my key already in the lock, my body paused with my held breath. I couldn't pretend that I hadn't arrived at the apartment building in Lisbon where I was just a few nights into my two-week visit. I peered through the window into the vestibule of the building, a sanctuary of fake marble tiles on the other side of the green metal door. A cold and dark space, and yet at once it appeared so inviting. How I wished I was on the other side of that door and heading up the stairs toward the security of comfort and familiarity.

It had only been two days since I had sat in that vestibule waiting for my Airbnb host to come home. It was daytime then—late morning—and the front door was open to give passers-by access to the shop on the ground floor. I had lugged my suitcase up three steep flights of stairs to the apartment.

It was dark in the stairwell, and I sweated right through the clothes I had been wearing for eighteen hours. When I left the United States, I was proud that my suitcase was so light—12 whole pounds below the maximum limit—but on that stairwell, it was a monstrosity, a symbol of my American gluttony and greed.

I found the third floor and stood at a crossroads of two doors, one on the left and one on the right. The one on the left wasn't addressed in any way, so I turned right and tapped the wood with my knuckles. A man opened the door. "Airbnb?" I asked.

"No," he said quickly before closing the door and securing the latch.

I descended back to the main floor and sat on the marble stairs, ignoring the glances of others who left or entered the building. Across the street, I saw the reflection of my building in the windows of another. The doorway cast a shadow, and I couldn't see myself unless I lingered on the sidewalk. Once inside the vestibule, I disappeared. On the street now, with you just at my elbow, there was too much darkness to be any kind of reflection in that window.

The minutes had passed slowly that first day in the stairwell. I shifted, adjusted a book on my knees, and tried to keep reading a collection of essays that was far smarter than I could ever write.

It was in that spot I learned my first Portuguese word—*desculpe*—"sorry" or "excuse me" when a woman carrying her own suitcase bumped me with it as she took the steps one at a time. I decided I had trespassed long enough, and I followed her out the door and onto the sun-drenched sidewalk.

I tried to wander, but my suitcase prevented me from going very far. We were limited to a four-block radius as the curving sidewalks turned into more stairs that extended a block up to the next street. I stopped for gelato and searched in vain for Wi-Fi to see if I could reach out to my Airbnb host. I tried to send a message but couldn't be certain that it had gone through. Even if it had, my phone wasn't cooperating well enough to receive a response. I finished my gelato, chucked the cup into a bin, and kept walking.

I found myself in a tourist section of the neighborhood, where shop after shop tried to entice the sidewalk crowd with its souvenirs. A waiter flashed a menu at me and gestured toward a table on the patio. Sure, I thought. It was a better option than sitting in a stairwell. Consumption would guarantee me a seat.

I drank two glasses of rose wine (Mateus: the original), and suddenly I was drunk in Lisbon. Drunk and tired and hot and homeless, and I longed for a place to sleep other than an airplane. I ordered a margherita pizza and gave an enthusiastic acceptance when the waiter asked me if I wanted another bottle of rose wine. For 6.95 euro, how could I say no? This is why, I thought, the homeless spend their money on booze. What other moment is there but the moment of right now?

I checked my watch to find that it was only 2 p.m. Nobody gets home from work at 2 p.m. to let his guest into his apartment. And so I took another swallow of wine. Four more hours of living as a little puppet of the city, desolate in a foreign country. Four hours, at the very least.

This, like everything else erroneous in my life, felt like punishment. But what had been my wrongdoing?

On the dark sidewalk, my key in the door, I felt a different kind of panic. I couldn't turn and walk the other way without fighting the key from the lock, obviously announcing to you that I was nervous and that you were in control. I also couldn't just ignore you and unlock the door because the key needed adjusting, wriggling, a process that required my concentration, and I couldn't concentrate on the lock while also keeping an eye on you.

I asked you to repeat your question. I shook my head that I couldn't help you, regardless. I don't smoke, I wanted to say, but maybe you asked me something else, your gentle accented voice difficult to hear over the adrenaline banging against my eardrums. Maybe you had a different question or other intentions. Maybe I didn't hear you because I hadn't wanted to.

Maybe you saw me fidget, my eyes dancing from you to the lock, you to the lock, and you put your hands up in front of you and said, "I'm not a bad boy," and you smiled, and there was a moment between us for me to consider your declaration. "I'm from Greece," you said, nodding sheepishly. Your country was facing some economic trouble, and maybe that was why you had to emphasize that you weren't there at that moment to cause *me* any trouble. Maybe all you really wanted was to just borrow a lighter.

You asked me where I'm from as I went back to fumbling with the key. You moved past me and were no longer within the space I occupied in front of the door, no longer a perceived threat.

"Mich—United States," I mumbled. I almost couldn't speak, couldn't say the words that I had said to strangers every day since I arrived, claiming the land of my home place.

"Ah," you said, all-knowingly. "America." You started to turn away but swung halfway back toward me before leaving. "Goodnight," you said, and then you were gone, and I was quickly inside the building's entry, the door latching heavily behind me, the sound of a prison cell closing.

I thought of you later that week as I felt the eyes of the three construction workers on me while I held my place on the sidewalk; they were seated on either side of cobbled limestone,

　　　　　　　　　　　　　　　　　　　　　　　MELISSA GRUNOW

taking a break in the shade. I saw your face, animated in empathy, when one of them called, "Hello!" then proceeded to follow me after I ignored him.

I was lost in Bairro Alto, far from my heavy front door with the decisive lock and even farther from the St. George Castle that I had planned to tour that afternoon. I squinted my eyes behind my sunglasses as I heard the *swoosh-swoosh* of the man's jeans gain on me, and I couldn't decide if I should turn and face him or run. Even under the relentless sun on a Sunday afternoon, I felt trapped, simultaneously isolated and exposed. To my right I saw tall, tall flights of concrete steps leading to another unknown street, and to my left were shops and restaurants closed down until Monday morning. Even in the open air, I was trapped.

I remembered the space you gave me on the street; the more alarmed I felt, the more you backed away, your interaction prompted by a simple, innocent request. Behind me, the man continued calling, "Hello, hello, lady, hello," and I heard his companions laughing in the distance I created between us. I wanted to get away, but I didn't walk faster and I didn't run, just like I didn't run from you when I really had nowhere else to go.

When he finally stopped following me, he didn't say goodbye, he wasn't polite like you or dismissive like the man who approached Corey and me on the street during our last night in Lisbon, his hand open, a small bag of hash—or was it a large bag of marijuana?—cradled in his palm. That man said nothing, just offered up an opportunity to experience the city in a new way. Corey turned to me, her eyebrows raised, a did-you-see-that? smirk on her face, and then the man was gone, and the moment was gone before either of us could waive a hand to decline.

At 4:30 in the morning, I confronted three men outside the Baixa/Chiado Metro stop who tried to talk to us, Corey and me, but we were drunk, it was late, and we weren't interested, so we kept walking. One spoke to me directly, his voice lilting with a Portuguese accent. I turned to answer him, and his hand was unbuttoning his jeans, his other hand on the zipper, and I saw the face of a demon when he smiled, his friends laughing.

We were not laughing.

Corey nudged my elbow, her face toward the dark corner that we needed to turn to go home. I barely heard her mumble, "Let's go," her voice buried by my screaming every American curse words I had in my lexicon. She could slink away at that moment, just like I had wanted to do when you spoke to me outside my apartment, but I was ignited and ready to fight, as though I had to justify being in the same space as them.

Would you have laughed if it was your friend on the street in the middle of the night in the middle of Lisbon in the middle of the Metro entryway who made an assaulting gesture at two American women? I want to believe by now that a man who was concerned with my reaction to him wouldn't be the same man who would start to pull his dick out, amused by the anger and rage he provoked.

In the minutes that followed after you approached me on the street, I wondered if I did the right thing by responding to your requests with suspicion, by answering your questions with hesitation. I wondered if I overreacted, and I felt a little guilty that you had to declare your good intentions. Often, in the aftermath of anything, we regret what we did and what we didn't do. How rare it is that we hit the mark exactly.

MELISSA GRUNOW

DWELLING PLACE

*"One never reaches home, but wherever friendly paths
intersect the whole world looks like home for a time."*
—HERMANN HESSE, *DEMIAN*

"Do you smell that?" I asked.

Dave closed the door against the cold November night air behind him. He studied the yellow walls and textured ceiling of the living room, scanned over the cobwebs in the corners, the stains on the flattened carpeting. "Smell what?" he asked.

I inhaled again. It was subtle but evident. I wandered into the kitchen while taking giant breaths in through my nose until I was dizzy. I tossed the house key onto the counter and listened to it clang and then settle onto the outdated teal Formica. I would have to add it to my key ring later.

"I don't smell anything," Dave said, though he never did. Five years of heavy smoking at the poker table in the Las Vegas Palms Casino before moving back to Michigan had made sure of that.

A cheap, gel air freshener from a dollar store sat dried up on the counter. Once the smell of strawberries, it could no longer cover the distinctive odor of water damage, mildew, rot.

I hadn't noticed the odor while house hunting or during the home inspection. But I couldn't deny it now. It was all around us, like a damp dungeon slowly closing in.

Dave set the envelope of signed mortgage papers on the stove. I imagined clicking on the gas burner and watching them catch fire, my signature on the bottom of each page turning to ash and floating away, absolving me of any responsibility for something I wasn't sure I was ready to handle.

Maybe, I hoped. Maybe what the house just needed was a good cleaning. Maybe, what I knew was a serious something, would turn out to be a simple nothing.

~

"Maybe we should move," John said with his back to me as he chopped something on the counter.

We had lived in the two-bedroom cinderblock house owned by the university for two months, maybe less. Our mail had started catching up to us after we relocated from Michigan in August, and the post office was recognizing my name change after our wedding in May. We were finally starting to settle into a shared life.

I was sitting on the chipped tile floor in the kitchen while John prepared dinner, pausing the chopping knife every few minutes to complain about the poems written by classmates in his MFA workshop. As he described the cacophony rhythm and malapropisms of a poem titled "Doppelganger," I stopped listening right after he said something about how the writer couldn't pronounce "metonymy" correctly, so maybe she didn't know what it meant, either. I was twenty-one and just a few weeks into the first semester of my master's program in English. Although always a good student, I didn't know what "metonymy" meant, and I knew better than to ask him. He would chide me for it, I was certain. I made a mental note to also look it up later, along with the meaning of "doppelganger." It was another sign that maybe I wasn't ready for graduate school, after all.

A maintenance man popped his head in through the opened back door and said, "Can you flush the toilet three or four times?"

John turned back to the stove, so the task was on me. I sighed and wandered into the bathroom.

I had come home from class that evening just before the sun settled behind the tall palm trees to find sewage flooding shit and toilet paper down our driveway. The University Facilities Office explained the main pipe for the street ran through our backyard, and one of our neighbors must have flushed something that caused it to clog and then burst. They would send someone over right away. That someone was now working alone outside in the dark and needed to test a patch or a replacement by running waste water through it. He couldn't do two tasks as once, so I was enlisted to be his apprentice when I should have been writing an essay or looking up definitions of words I should already know.

I pushed the lever down on the toilet, watched the water swirl, and then pushed again. Sand and debris had backed up into the bowl but thinned out with each flush. I pulled the curtain closed on the bathtub to hide the brown ring of grit that would need to be scrubbed before we could use it again. I had to teach a composition class at eight o'clock the next morning to twenty-five wide-eyed freshmen who knew even less about the subject than I did. I already felt as though I was arriving unprepared each day dressed in cargo jeans and a polo shirt, my backpack heavy on my shoulders making it easy for anyone to mistake me for an undergraduate. I barely had any credibility in the classroom as it were. I couldn't show up unshowered, too.

John clattered pans in the kitchen and soon the smell of simmering garlic masked the neighborhood waste that was wafting up through the drains. I was both starving and nauseous, but still less concerned about eating dinner than I was with the maintenance man finishing whatever he needed to finish outside and for my husband to stop complaining about his class and with the excerpt from Chaucer I had to read for my literature class, fearing I probably wouldn't understand it and would have very little to contribute to group discussion the following week.

John slid two tightly rolled burritos onto a plate, topped them with jarred salsa and passed the plate to me. I gripped it with both hands and carried it to the living room where I sat cross-legged on the futon in front a television that didn't have cable. We hadn't yet accepted the inconveniences of the place, had barely grown accustomed to the swamp cooler in lieu of central A/C, our wall art stacked in a corner on the floor because we simply couldn't get a nail into the concrete walls. It was just for two years, we reasoned, at least until I finished my program. It was cheap, within walking distance to our classroom buildings, and big enough for the two of us. We signed the paperwork sight unseen because we didn't have the money to fly down and apartment search before our move. We liked the idea of a house with a yard and our own driveway. In our minds, it was the perfect solution for newlywed graduate students trying to pretend that we weren't living in poverty.

"Should I offer him some?" John whispered and nodded his head toward the window. We could hear the maintenance man digging around in the bed of a pickup truck for what would hopefully be the perfect tool, the ultimate solution to a problem we never could have predicted.

I shrugged. I had never been home while someone was repairing something on a rental, and I had never before rented a *house*. I didn't know the protocol.

John wrapped the burritos in tinfoil and brought them outside where the other man politely declined, holding his hand to his stomach and proclaiming something about being on a diet. John set them on the window ledge and said, "I'll leave them here in case you change your mind." He never was very good at taking no for an answer.

It was midnight before I could finally scrub out the inside of the tub with floral-scented all-purpose cleaner, even later before I crawled into bed and slept a restless sleep, the smell of the sewer pipe and chemically manufactured lilacs lingering in my nose.

In the morning, I stepped outside to walk to class while John was sleeping and saw that there were still traces of waste and rivulets from run-off etched into the dirt yard. The two burritos remained on the ledge, slightly flattened and swarming with fire ants.

Throughout the day, I was grateful to be away from the house as I spent the afternoon locked in the office I shared with two other graduate students and skimmed through as many pages of *The Wife of Bath* as I could. I underlined interesting passages and blindly marked up the margins, hoping someone else had done more reading than I had and would be able to carry the three-hour discussion.

When we first arrived in Las Cruces and were assigned a house on Poe Drive, I thought it was a kind of serendipitous sign from the universe; it couldn't just be coincidence that I was studying literature and living on the only street named after one of the most well-known writers in American history. I ignored the fact that I actually despised the Gothic period, particularly Poe's writing, and was resentful of being forced to memorize part of "The Raven" in sixth grade along with all of the conjugations of "to be" and the fifty states in alphabetical order.

In the evening, I strolled slowly toward the house in no hurry to be home. Our shared car was in the driveway, but that didn't mean John was home yet, and the darkness behind the closed curtains made me hopeful that I would have a few moments to myself.

As I approached the door, I saw the burritos were gone but the bits of waste and toilet paper on the ground were not. Instead, they had spent the day baking in the sun until they were a dried up brown smear along the edge of the driveway.

We weren't prepared for a house. We weren't prepared for a yard or any kind of yard maintenance. We didn't even own a shovel or a rake and there wasn't a place to store them if we did. We most certainly weren't prepared for a public health hazard in our sad, unkempt yard.

Locking the door behind me, I dropped my bag onto the futon and flipped a light switch to turn on a table lamp just in time to see a quarter-sized shadow scurry across the floor and behind the television stand.

"Shit," I muttered. Our previous place in Mount Pleasant, a saggy bungalow with tired shag carpeting, had a cricket infestation that had emerged in the spring and continued relentlessly through the summer. We packed carefully, checking boxes before filling them with our belongings and sealing them closed tightly with packing tape. No matter our care, a few must have slipped through, I told John when he arrived home an hour later.

"They aren't crickets," he said, shaking his head.

"No?"

"Nope."

"Then what?"

"Cockroaches." He paused for a moment as he kicked off his shoes. "I smashed a huge one on the wall in the kitchen last night."

"The kitchen?" I'd had enough. First the sewage and now cockroaches? Not to mention the hordes of fire ants, the useless yard, and a cinderblock box that resembled a bunker more than a house.

"Maybe we should move," he suggested again.

It would be my third move in six months. The house in Mount Pleasant was a brief stopover for me between living alone in my apartment and relocating to Las Cruces with my new husband. It was so hot throughout June and July that we had to sleep in the living room with the windows wide open and oscillating fans circulating thick air. The toilet seat was cracked, and it pinched my butt each time I sat on it. The shower was a plastic stall in the corner with low water pressure and no ventilation. I had only agreed to live there instead of my two-bedroom apartment because John convinced me the house was bigger, and we needed the space even though I was more settled and had more to move. I obliged because I wanted to be agreeable, a good wife. I endured it because it was temporary.

The university agreed to send someone to clean up the yard, but it was futile. In the days that followed, I would lay awake at night listening for the scuttling sounds of desert critters, and in the morning I would curse the tiny bathroom sink while I brushed my teeth or dried my hair, the humidity from the evaporative cooler an endless battle of frustration. All of this against the backdrop of John's growing litany of complaints, drawing my attention to the imperfections and the inconveniences of the house.

"Okay," I agreed after crushing a cockroach that had darted indoors while I was handing out candy to trick-or-treaters. "Let's move."

Our means of apartment-hunting were limited; very few rentals were listed on the Internet at that time, and those that we could find were often well out of our price range. Instead, finding a new place to live meant driving around in an unfamiliar town hoping to spot "For Rent" signs in lawns, skimming the classified ads in the newspaper, and relying on word of mouth. Most places we could afford were targeted toward undergraduate renters, which meant we could potentially end up living next door or across the hall from our students, a situation we definitely wanted to avoid. We were also limited by location; moving downtown or to the north end of the city meant a longer commute with a shared car.

I would come to know the apartment-hunting process well three years later when we were on the brink of divorce, and I can't say that it got easier on one income. All of the same situational factors applied, but I had learned that a money-saving place would likely mean older, grittier, and roach-infested. By then, I would be a desert transplant for four years, and I would know that, in fact, *every* home in Las Cruces had roaches, it was just some places had more and bigger bugs than others. I grew accustomed to maintaining a spotless household, keeping food tightly sealed or refrigerated, and footing the bill every two weeks for an exterminator. It was a good sign, I would discover, to find roaches belly up in the middle of the floor, their legs barely kicking as they succumbed to the nerve-damaging poison sprayed around the baseboards once a month. Roaches come out of their dark hiding places to die. As long as I scooped them up before they attracted other bugs, I was doing everything within my power to keep the pests at bay.

But when we decided to move out of the house on Poe Drive, I didn't know anything about the culture of desert bugs. Living in Michigan my whole life, cockroaches meant ramshackle dwelling places, overcrowded low-income city housing, and poverty. For me, roaches were a stigma, a

MELISSA GRUNOW

representation of something I was trying to escape, to outrun, and to deny.

We insisted we needed a two-bedroom apartment until our friend Kenny showed us the one-bedroom place on Fairway Drive, a few miles north of campus. It was part of a single-story complex owned by his boyfriend's family, and aside from a few working professionals, was inhabited mostly by divorced or widowed elderly women. It had wall-to-wall Berber carpeting, a sliding glass door leading to a concrete patio, a larger—though outdated—kitchen, interior brick, and best of all, central A/C. It was the same square footage as the cinderblock house on Poe Drive, but more spread out and one less room. While at the top end of our price range, Nick gave us a discount and waived the security deposit. It was the best we would be able to do, and we knew it.

I gave notice to the university housing office that day, and we moved into the apartment within a week. The large space filled quickly as we loaded two desks, a bed, and a dresser into the bedroom and filled an entire living room wall with bookcases and the television stand. We had big plans to set up a patio set in the back, but never got beyond foldable camping chairs that we only brought out when we had friends over. Sandwiched between two other units, we had very little natural light, but it had free cable—thanks to the landlord—and was generally quiet. The landscaping was well-maintained by their gardener Jesús, and there was never, ever a burst sewer pipe. It looked middle class, and while living there, we *felt* middle class. We weren't graduate students or twenty-some-things or newlyweds or two people trying to figure it out. We were adults.

Out of all the places we lived while together, we stayed in that place the longest (nearly two years) and fought with each other the most during that time. We thought that being confined to the same shared spaces was part of the problem, so when a two-bedroom unit opened up in the same complex, we moved in, even though we could barely afford it. I was out of graduate school by then and working full-time, and John was in the third and final year of his MFA program. He set the second bedroom up as his office, his desk facing the door as if he were a receptionist, his computer screen always hidden from my view. I never asked him why or what he was doing when he sat at that desk late into the night, long after I had to go to sleep. I always assumed it was important, school-related, and career-building. I always assumed that the things he did were in our shared best interest.

It wasn't long before the complaints about the two-bedroom apartment started. It had worn carpeting that never looked clean even after we vacuumed, he said. The kitchen cabinets were old and coated with a layer of fingerprint grime at the corners, he said. It faced the parking lot allowing visitors to stare in through our patio door, he said. There wasn't enough closet space, he said. We had gotten a second cat and there was nowhere logical to put a second litter box, he said. It was too expensive and didn't even have the character of southwest architecture, he said. The bathroom fan was too loud, everything was beige, our bedroom window faced the walkway to the back apartments, the parking lot was always packed, it was a long way to carry groceries, the front door had a sticky latch, we had to share coin-operated washers and dryers with the other tenants, and the stove was electric, not gas, he said.

"You know what else I don't like about this place?" he would ask, and I braced myself for newly realized grievances, nodding along whether I agreed or not. I did think it was too expensive. We were running out of money faster than before I started working full-time. I had thought graduating and getting a job meant an immediate improvement in our comfort level, but it mostly stayed the same, and even dipped a little when I had to start repaying my student loans. I regretted leaving the one-bedroom apartment simply for the cost difference, even though I appreciated the extra space in the larger unit.

Before long, John would come home with a newspaper tucked under his arm, sit at the dining table and read through the classifieds. He was graduating soon, but he didn't have any job prospects. Even though his graduate assistant stipend wasn't much, it was still better than no salary at all. Moving would cost us money: a rental truck, security deposit, disconnecting and reconnecting the utilities, and it didn't make sense to me to spend it when the future was so uncertain. Although the apartment was pricey, we were settled there and knew how much to budget for each month. A new place would mean an adjustment in living expenses, as it always did. No matter how many times we had moved to save money, we always seemed to pay more. John was a spender who liked to make it look like we had money with an endless cycle of new purchases. We kept our grievances with each other to ourselves. We didn't really fight anymore, but we also weren't happy.

While I dressed up in trousers and button-down shirts every day for my job in an office, John stayed home to read books and write his thesis. At the end of the day, I would often find him in the same threadbare basketball shorts and T-shirt from that morning, unshowered, hair a mess, sitting in an arm chair with one leg crossed over the other, a pillow and book in his lap, the television on. How he could write in front of the TV, I never understood. New receipts from the day's purchases would be resting on the counter in front of the microwave. He may not have had time to shower, but he found time to shop. It was something we needed, he would justify. We always needed more than we had.

"Do you remember Nena?" he asked me one evening as we settled into our after-dinner routine.

"Sure," I said. Nena was a first-year MFA student who I had met at parties with other writers.

"She's looking for someone to take over her lease."

I nodded. I knew where this conversation was going. We talked about moving nearly every night, and it was more frequent the closer John got to graduating.

He told me about the place she was renting from a previous MFA student now living in Ireland. The house was in La Mesa, a neighboring town on the outskirts of Las Cruces.

"Okay," I conceded. "We can go look at it."

That Friday, I sat in the passenger seat and watched as the neighborhood outside my window turned into Old Mesilla, then irrigated fields, and then nothing. After about fifteen minutes I asked if we were close. I hadn't been anywhere in New Mexico that was more than a fifteen-minute drive without getting on the freeway. How much further could it be?

It was late afternoon when we turned onto the two-lane road lined with trees on both sides, trees so tall that they filtered the sun through their leaves, the reflections dancing on the windshield. I hadn't seen trees like that since leaving Michigan.

"They're pecan groves," John said.

"Pecans? As in nuts?"

He laughed, but not because he found the question funny. "Yeah."

How was that possible? Pecans, while popular, were outrageously expensive. Yet they grew right here; the trees continued for miles. I felt myself relax and settle into the seat. A longer commute wouldn't be so bad if it meant I had to pass through the groves twice a day.

We parked on the dirt road next to the house because there wasn't a driveway. Nena met us at the gate and explained that there actually wasn't a key for the front door, so she always used the back. The yard was small, but quaint, with a pergola and seating. John and Nena chattered about the space, having people over, enjoying the evenings outside, something we couldn't do on our apartment patio that faced the parking lot and the street.

The back door opened into a large kitchen with lavender-colored walls. Nena showed off the spacious pantry, the countertops, and the natural light spilling in through the windows, though we were still shielded from the street thanks to the privacy fence encasing the yard. The kitchen opened into a large dining room with a doorway to an L-shaped hallway to the right. The only bathroom was at the short end of the hallway, next to a laundry and storage room, and off the long end of the hallway were two bedrooms with a shared closet and a living room. The floors were wall-to-wall ceramic tile and above our heads in the hallway was the vent for the swamp cooler on the roof.

The house was old, a cinderblock structure, white with bright blue trim and landscaped with cactuses. It had southern New Mexico character, three bedrooms, and the rent was cheaper than our apartment.

John loved it.

Nena explained that while the house had a physical address, there was no postal service in the neighborhood, but we could rent a P.O. Box at the general store two blocks away. She drove us around the neighborhood and pointed out the lone Mexican restaurant, the fields framed by irrigation ditches, the house on the corner with chickens and the one down the street with a donkey. The homes ranged from trailers to cinder-block and plaster to what resembled makeshift lean-tos made from steel plates. The house next door had a large front yard full of furniture and other household items; stray cats meandered about, skinny and haunted, meowing defensively.

Throughout the weekend, John brought up the house in conversation often, working to convince me that it was the place for us. He described it as relaxing and better in ways that I couldn't see. "It's more authentic," he said. "Like we *actually* live in New Mexico."

I knew John was miserable. I knew it even more so than he did. He tried to find joy in shopping but was never content with the purchases. We replaced desks, couches, our bed, various tables and furniture pieces to better meet his liking, but the novelty of the new wore off quickly.

Maybe the misery was because of the apartment after all. It was the only factor that had stayed the same. John loved the house in La Mesa, and if we could just find a place that didn't make him miserable, then maybe we could be happy with each other. Keeping our marriage together meant another move, possibly dozens more, until John could settle into a place that he couldn't blame for his despondency.

We moved on what felt like the hottest day of the year. As I packed, I discretely filled trash bags with old pantry items, closet fillers, and miscellaneous odds and ends and tossed them into the trash to cut down on the number of packed boxes and clutter in our new home. We had a few friends who graciously helped us load the truck and unload it after the thirty-minute drive to the new house, all of us sweating through our clothes and complaining relentlessly about the heat.

MELISSA GRUNOW

Deanna and I loaded the bed of her pickup and got to the house first while her boyfriend and John piled furniture into the moving truck. John and I had been bickering all morning, and I was relieved to have some time away from him.

"I wonder why they picked the name La Mesa," Deanna said.

"What do you mean?" I let the hot wind dry my sweaty hair as we passed through the groves. Her truck didn't have air conditioning.

"It means 'the table.' Is it on a plateau?" Deanna was a geologist and always naming different rock formations and natural wonders of the desert.

"I have no idea," I said. "All I see are fields and groves."

"And gang tags." She pointed to an abandoned building layered with graffiti before turning off the main road and onto our street.

The inside of the empty house echoed as Deanna and I walked from room to room. With all of Nena's furniture removed, we could see corners of plaster crumbling onto the floor, sooty shadows from overuse of candles, and closets still full of extra paint cans, extra building materials, and tools. We had far less storage than we thought.

"How do you suppose I turn this on?" I pointed to the swamp cooler vent above my head.

Deanna turned a dial on the wall. "Maybe this?"

Nothing. No familiar click. No wind tunnel effect. No cooling air.

"Maybe it needs to be serviced," she said.

Serviced? I wondered. *Shouldn't it just work?* It was May, summertime in New Mexico, and the house was already getting warmer. Without some way of cooling it down, sleep would be impossible. How had Nena survived here?

When John arrived with Erik in the moving truck, I told him about the swamp cooler. He mumbled something about emailing the homeowner in Ireland once our internet was connected, and we immediately got to work unloading.

Boxes piled into rooms. Furniture settled against walls and into corners. Little by little, the truck became empty and we had a new home to settle into.

That night we slept little and fitfully, the fans ineffective against the heat. I woke up early the next morning to unpack the kitchen, a task that always took the longest but cleared the most boxes. I opened and closed cabinet doors to assess the space. Our cats roamed cautiously, meowing in wonder at the tile beneath their feet until they curled up on the back of the couch to watch the new world take shape outside the large front window.

My mind was quiet while I worked. I was accustomed to this process by now. John always insisted we move, and I was always up early to unpack when we did. I welcomed the silence, though, the quiet of the house. There wasn't any traffic on our little dirt road, and though we could see the neighbors, we couldn't really hear them. Maybe it was too early in the day for our new world to be stirring, or maybe we had found a place of peace and serenity.

I let my shoulders relax and let the newspaper wrapping the dishes fall to the floor in piles around me. My fingertips, stained with ink, left prints on the outside of the plates. I didn't bother to care. The home was rustic and charming; a little smudging wasn't going to hurt anyone.

It wasn't long before the cockroaches came out to play. This time they were alive and brazen, darting across the tile floor of a brightly lit room. Often they were too fast for us, but not fast enough to outrun the cats who supplemented their daily bowl of dry food with an ongoing hunt for the desert bugs that always found their way in. Even after we had an exterminator

MELISSA GRUNOW

come once a week, the cockroaches were still everywhere, sometimes belly up and twitching, other times clinging to the side of a wall and watching us go about our lives. They were all sizes, different shapes, some brown, some a deep black. The brown ones had wings and would flutter from a doorframe or a hidden perch and mill around on whatever surface they chose. We would prepare meals and package leftovers at the same time we made up our plates to avoid leaving food on the counter. Everything went into the refrigerator or airtight glass containers in the pantry. If it could be chewed through or burrowed into, it was tossed. Even then, the cockroaches were relentless. It was worse than the cricket infestation in Mount Pleasant and far worse than anything we had endured living in what we soon realized was a luxury apartment.

A walk from our house to the post office and back often revealed why. Like our neighbor next door, the houses around us had lawns overrun with old couches, chairs, wood piles, and car parts, a breeding ground for critters and housing for the stray cats that would squeal in agony outside our window at night as they fought or mated. They had missing ears and poorly healed broken limbs and eye infections and mange. We were grateful for them simply because they probably kept the inevitable mouse and rat influx under control even though the cats themselves were visibly suffering.

Soon enough, the novelty of the house wore off, even for John. Heavy rains in August soaked our street until it was a muddy sludge that swallowed our feet and left the hems of my pants stained and shoes ruined. It was a precarious adventure to drive down the street after dark if a chicken was bolting through the neighborhood. At one point, someone's pigs escaped their pen, and at least fifteen of them roamed in the glimmer of my headlights, nosing in the trash cans and knocking over makeshift fences to root in yards. Sometimes, it was a lone goat that was completely unfazed by a honking horn or flashing lights that interrupted my drive home.

The washing machine would often drain improperly and flood the hallway, sending the cats to higher ground, crying that their beds were wet and they couldn't get to their food bowls. As the summer wore on and the swamp cooler ran almost incessantly, the doors began to swell and stick in their frames, the loose plaster continued to fall and pile up behind furniture, and the pages of our books fanned out and crinkled from the damp air.

Most notably, John still wasn't happy. He had graduated and was teaching a summer class that covered only a fraction of our expenses. He was picky about where he worked, the nature of his job. Every interview came with it a slew of reasons why he could never work *there*, could never be expected to do *that*. This was the same man who had delivered sandwiches for pathetic tips while we were dating. Now that he had two master's degrees, he was suddenly particular about how he earned his money.

He started talking about moving again, this time suggesting that we leave New Mexico entirely. If he couldn't find a job doing what he wanted, maybe we should consider his family in Colorado or embark on the next new adventure together.

After all, he wasn't happy, he admitted finally. What he didn't realize, though, was neither was I, and it had nothing to do with the inconveniences of where we lived. It had everything to do with the slow dissolve of our marriage.

After six months in La Mesa, we did move again. Except this time, he moved into his own apartment, and I found a place of my own near my job downtown. We divided belongings as we packed them into separate boxes, wrote our own names on them, and taped them up tightly in hopes of keeping the bugs out. During my lunch break, I opened a new bank account in just my name and began depositing my checks there. I removed him as an authorized user from my credit card, and he completed appropriate paperwork to release me as cosigner on his car loan. We divided our savings, the balance of our joint checking account, kept the same books and CDs that we brought into the marriage, and each took a cat. There was no fighting; there was no bitter resentment. Neither felt like we had lost anything, and yet both of us felt like we were walking away from everything.

———

"I just want to take out a wall," Dave said. We were wandering through the fifteenth, maybe twentieth, vacant house within my price range. When I had first been pre-approved for a mortgage, my lender commented that he wasn't sure what I would find for that amount, so maybe I should consider a condo. To me, a condo was no different than an apartment; in fact, many apartment buildings had converted to occupant-owned, rather than company-owned dwellings. If I was going to purchase a place to live, it was going to be a detached home, not a space that shared walls with strangers.

I rolled my eyes at Dave but said nothing. He told everyone we were buying a house, but the truth was I was buying a house and it was implied that we would move into it together. I felt unsettled in the apartment we were sharing, a banal resemblance to the two-bedroom in Las Cruces that John and I had shared before moving to La Mesa. Before I met Dave, I had my own one-bedroom flat on the second floor of a house that I moved into shortly after returning to Michigan. It was comfortable and affordable, but not big enough for two. When Dave and I decided to move in together, I relinquished the space that I loved for a place that fit both of us. Very quickly, though, I came to understand the shared apartment space wasn't my space. It created a loathsome commute of stop-and-go traffic so frustrating that I sometimes stayed late at work just to avoid driving home.

The decision to buy a house came quickly and without much pause. The housing market in the Detroit area had collapsed. Underwater mortgages forced people into foreclosure, and houses sat vacant, some for years. Once-thriving neighborhoods were overrun with "For Sale" signs, and the government was offering tax incentives for first-time buyers.

If I was ever going to own a house, this was the time to do it.

I was cautious not to max out my pre-approved loan amount, and instead focused on houses that were listing for significantly less. Dave, on the other hand, wanted both a prize and a project house, something to show off to his friends and family.

Initially, he didn't want to live in the house I ended up buying. It's ugly, he said, and with its outdated aluminum siding and crumbling front porch, he was right. Those things, I tried to explain, were cosmetic and something I could have fixed with the tax incentive. I don't like the street, he said. It's too industrial. I countered that it was in a typical neighborhood just like everything else we looked at. Well, it's in a bad area, he said. He wanted us to look more north, closer to our apartment, closer to his work, and further from Detroit. He couldn't see the house through its shortcomings. All I could see was potential.

So I bought it.

"You really can't smell that?" I asked as we stood in the kitchen and looked around the room making mental notes of which task to tackle first.

MELISSA GRUNOW

He shook his head. "Didn't you want to lower those cabinets?" he asked instead.

The cabinets were sized to go under a soffit, but instead were hung with the tops butting up against the ceiling. I could barely reach the first shelf of each one, and the gross amount of distance hovering above the countertops made them look ridiculous.

Taking down cabinets is easy. It's really just a few stud screws holding them in place. They were heavy, but there were only four of them. Dave got the drill, I got the ladder, and together we maneuvered each one off the wall and onto the floor, taking care to not let them slip, to fall, to smash into pieces on the creaky hardwood.

As we removed the fourth and final cabinet, I saw the water damage that had eaten through the drywall in the ceiling and turned the attic insulation from pink to black. An old leak from the upstairs bathroom sink had found its way deep into the ceiling above us, and we came face-to-face with the very smell that I had confronted when I first walked into the house.

I didn't think at first about the cost of repairs, the need for mold removal, that the hole in the ceiling would lead to weeks of removing drywall, rewiring the outlets, replacing the countertop, the sink, even the garbage disposal, as one discovery led to another necessary repair. I didn't think about what it would mean to live without a functioning kitchen, to cut corners on low-grade building materials that would need to be replaced entirely when the kitchen was professionally remodeled six years later. I didn't think about how the project would divide us as a couple, how Dave would reveal through behavior and attitude that since I was the one earning the equity, I should be the one to foot the bill for all tools and materials, even though he told everyone it was *our* house.

What I thought about was the desire to run, to bolt from my life. To walk away from this commitment the same way I had walked away from the others in an attempt to save something that didn't have merit. I wanted to leave that place and be gone. I had spent so much time in temporary dwelling places that I started to feel like a transient. My independence wasn't freedom but a necessity for survival.

Of course, the water damage was dealt with, but it took time and money that I hadn't planned to spend. There were more problems as the months dragged on into years, but I endured it, and so did the house. Dave, however, did not. Within a year, he was gone, and I learned to get comfortable with power tools and online tutorials whenever a big something turned out to be a manageable nothing. Sometimes I had to call on professionals or seek out knowledgeable friends for guidance, but it was never so daunting that I abandoned what was mine. In the end, though, it was more than a house—it was my permanent home—and when something broke I came to accept that there was nobody there to fix it but me.

MENG LI SHA

*"Human speech is like a cracked kettle on which we tap
crude rhythms for bears to dance to, while we long
to make music that will melt the stars."*
—GUSTAVE FLAUBERT, *MADAME BOVARY*

Nikki stands in the sweltering cafeteria, clutching her metal tray. "Why did this have to happen to me?" The corners of her mouth curl upward in amused exasperation.

On Nikki's tray is an unrecognizable chopped vegetable concoction, some rice, and—to her dismay—a boiled duck head.

Children scurry to find seats at long metal picnic tables. Nikki and I slide onto a bench next to one another and set our trays on the table. My right knee cracks, and I'm reminded that my ankles are still swollen from the fourteen-hour plane ride after enduring a thirty-hour travel delay. I had finally arrived after 10 p.m. the night before and was up at 6 a.m. to teach my first class at The Changxing Victoria Foreign Language School, an English summer camp for Chinese elementary school children in the Zhejiang province.

"I'm not eating that," Nikki whispers to me as she picks up her chopsticks and pokes the empty eye socket of the offending duck head.

"Are you supposed to?" I ask. "Maybe it's a garnish. Like parsley."

She gives me a look and attempts to eat her rice, the individual bits slipping out of her chopsticks and back onto her tray.

Around us, the students are shoveling food into their mouths, pieces of rice, vegetable, and meat falling back onto the table as their voices rise in a chorus above their heads, along with steam from our collective sweat. The heat continues to build in the room, the air so heavy that I'm full even before I've taken my first bite. Across from me, Kate picks up a duck foot from her tray and nibbles on the toes; her head is tilted slightly and propped up on her small hand, the elbow resting on the table. Her English is quite limited, but she quickly becomes my favorite student because her face is full of expressions. She's light enough for me to lift up over my head, so I give her the nickname Carry-on Kate.

"Teacher, excuse me."

I turn and see a girl standing next to me at the end of the table. Her hair is pulled into a tight ponytail at the crown of her head. She has a big smile and animated features.

"My name is Jenny." All of the students already have English names that they've picked off a list that will stick with them in English classes through college. Names like Grace, Kate, Judy, Sandra, Rick, Penny, and Sylvia are typical, but there are less conventional choices such as Yo-Yo, Cookie, Happy, and Madonna, as pop culture America has made its way to the other side of the world.

Jenny taps her chin and rolls her eyes upward as she searches for her words. "Um, what do you like to do on the weekend?"

Her question puzzles me at first. There is no weekend in China, at least not the kind we're accustomed to in the U.S. Our teaching schedule doesn't permit us a weekend either, just a day off every six or eight days to go on excursion.

"I like to spend time with friends and read books," I finally say. "What do you like to do on the weekend?"

"I like to go to the movies," she says, and smiles a toothy grin.

This brief interaction gives me an extensive amount of insight into what some of the children may already know and how much English they can speak. Jenny is advanced because she can form conversational sentences without prompting. She also doesn't seem to be experiencing the same shyness and hesitation with us foreign visitors as the other students, who spent the morning quietly staring and occasionally giggling in between recitation of English vocabulary, definitions, and sentences.

Back in the classroom, Nikki and I stumble around each other and make quick decisions as to who will cover which aspect of the lesson. She's a college student, and I'm a college instructor, even though we're only six years apart. I have more than five years of experience in front of the classroom, and she has none. We're strangers, essentially, having met just a few times before this teaching abroad opportunity. There are polite suggestions, nervous laughter, and a flexible mentality. We may not know yet how to work together, but we have to give the appearance that we know what we're doing, as the room is filled with little faces eager for an English education.

We teach the children the different words for family members: mother, father, grandma, grandpa, sister, brother. But this is the age of the one-child law, so they don't have siblings and refer to their cousins as brother or sister instead. The students repeat our slow pronunciations, write the word and definition in their notebooks, and raise their hands eagerly when we ask for volunteers to recite back to us.

After vocabulary, Nikki and I ask our students to work in small groups and come up with Chinese names for us. They scramble to rearrange their chairs, open their notebooks, and start to sketch characters in varying designs while we circulate the room. They're conversing quickly, arguing over which combination is better, which letters sound the most like our English names. Each group takes turns going to the front of the room and writing their choice on the board, then they present what each character sounds like and its meaning. For me they choose Meng Li Sha, and for Nikki, Nih-ka.

After school, Billie and Vivian, the class's Chinese teachers and our guides while we're in Changxing, approach us. "We go to Rick's house for dinner."

I turn and scan the children, trying to locate Rick. He's a tiny boy with glasses and a big smile, who Nikki has nicknamed "Chicken Little." He is one of the quietest children in class, so it surprises me that he will be our host for the evening.

We ride the bus into town, and Billie and Vivian flag down a taxi. They push Nikki and me inside with Rick, who is squished in between us. They say something to him in Mandarin, close the door, and the cab drives away.

"Nikki," I say through clenched teeth. "We're in a cab in China with a child."

Nikki's eyes are wide. She nods and lets out a nervous laugh. It's our first full day in a foreign city in which we don't know the language, our child escort doesn't know English, and we're driving further and further away from the familiarity of our hotel, and we don't even know the name of it.

The taxi pulls to the side of the road just outside tall apartment buildings. Rick hands the driver money and points to the door. I climb out and he follows, then stands on the sidewalk clutching his school bag.

"Rick, do you live here? Are your teachers coming?"

He shakes his head and looks away while saying something quietly in Mandarin. It's clear he doesn't understand me.

He waits and watches the road until another cab pulls up, and Billie and Vivian climb out. I look at Nikki and we both relax our shoulders. It would be an utter embarrassment if we had been left wandering around in downtown Changxing on our first full day in China.

"Come inside." Vivian leads us into a building, up three flights of stairs, and into the apartment. She instructs us to remove our shoes and slip on house shoes that are lined up neatly by the door in all different sizes. It's customary to wear something on your feet while inside someone's home, just not the shoes that you wear outside.

Nikki and I sit awkwardly next to each other on the firm and boxy couch. Rick sets two tall glasses with tea leaves in the bottom on the table in front of us. He fills each glass with boiling water, and the leaves swirl with the pour, turning the liquid to a pale green. I pick up my glass to take a sip and have to set it back down almost immediately. It's too hot to hold, let alone to drink.

Vivian hands each of us a round piece of fruit covered in a hard shell and shows us how to peel it. With the shell removed, the fruit is a bulbous gel, much like the inside of a grape, but sweeter. We ask what it's called, but neither Billie nor Vivian knows the name in English.

The language differences between us and Rick's family are so obvious that we can't even muster small talk because it all needs to be translated. We know it would be rude to just talk to each other, or to just talk to Billie and Vivian, so we don't talk at all. I'm stiff with social discomfort. I need something to do.

Rick's mother says something to Vivian, and she stands up quickly from her seat on the bamboo floor. "Come this way," she says.

We gather around a table and learn to stuff and fold wontons that Rick's mother boils in a large pot. Rick's father is stern and quiet until he smiles, and he is relentless in showing Nikki how to fold the wontons correctly so the filling doesn't ooze out from the folds. She clutches the wonton in front of her face and laughs with her head back while Rick's father repeatedly taps her shoulder to give her instructions once again.

Our days in China quickly fall into a pattern of teaching, meeting up with our students for dinner most nights—either in their homes or at restaurants—and occasionally spending time in town with Billie and Vivian, shopping and wandering the city, crossing over bridges where the river below shoots water into the air full of colored lights, the patterns dancing in the moonlight. Even as dusk approaches, there is no relief from the heat.

I'm in an urban jungle and the natives stare at my pinkish skin and red hair, a freak among homogeny. I'm also bigger than most of the men—in height and in stature—my limbs thick and heavy, my hips wide. In China I resemble a freshly picked cherry—red, round, and warm to the touch. We Americans are so obviously American. We can't help ourselves. But we don't expect to get stared at, photographed, and stared at some more. I meet the eyes of those who stare, but they don't look away. They keep their eyes focused on me as they steer their mopeds down the street with no regard for getting in the way of others. The only traffic law in Changxing is "Me first!" as scooters and cars fight for road space, riding their horn the whole way.

Initially, I scowl back and stare harder; after the first week, though, I smile, wave, flash peace signs, or just shrug it off. Vivian and Billie tell us that they've never had foreign visitors in Changxing, at least not from what they can remember. Nikki and I are an anomaly, the equivalent of little green men

MELISSA GRUNOW

walking down our street back home. If that happened, would we stare? Of course we would.

The smells in the street are made up of what I later learned was called Chinese five-spice powder, best described as a combination of burnt plastic, moth balls, and a sprinkling of old garlic. It's rubbed into flat pieces of beef that some of the families serve to us when we dine in their homes. The first time I tried it, I raised the piece to my nose, smelling it and studying its texture. It's cut in such a way that I don't recognize it as it curls slightly at the edges, dangling on the end of my chopsticks. I don't want it, but I eat it anyway to be polite, and wake up from a deep sleep later that night to throw it all up in the bathroom.

I would periodically smell that same spice as it wafted off the carts of street vendors while we wandered the city at night with Billie and Vivian. The bile would curdle in my throat, and I would stop, look around, and try to identify the culprit. I would turn to Nikki and shake my head, and she knew instantly that I had to move away, my hand over my nose.

Each day in the classroom centers on a different theme, the English taught in the context of American culture. Topics include money and shopping, food, school, holidays, sports. On sports day, we take the students outside and teach them relay games, including sponge toss which then turns into a water fight.

Nikki walks up behind Ramiz—another one of the American teachers—and dumps a bottle of water on his head.

He turns and points at her as she runs away. "Get Miss Nikki!"

The children pursue the chase as she weaves through cars in the small parking lot. Ramiz catches her and holds her still as the children douse her with water. There is a subtle flirtation between the two of them that gets more apparent each time they are together. Nikki has a love interest in the U.S. who won't commit, a guy who treats her like she is all that matters in the world as long as no one else is around. She is frustrated and confused and Ramiz's flirtations in a foreign country are a welcomed distraction.

There is a small pond next to the school where children fill their water bottles and chase after one another, soaking their clothes in the process. Emma walks up to me with a big smile on her face, and I smile back, just as she tosses the contents of her water bottle in my face, flooding my eyes and my mouth with pond scum. I am certain I have contracted dysentery or malaria, that I will go blind, that death is imminent. My mascara runs down my face as I rub my eyes and walk back to the school. Dick—the best English-speaking student in my class—takes my hand and leads me to a bench. He shouts in Mandarin at the students who approach me with full water bottles, while shielding me with a pink umbrella. The children back away, mortified that I am hurt or sad or something other than smiling while singing songs and clapping like usual. Dick is protective because he thinks I'm crying, and I smile to show him that I'm okay, that it's just the protozoans making my eyes water, all the while hoping my blurry vision is just my overreacting imagination.

Later that week, Nikki and I meet Dick's mother and some of his extended family for dinner out in the country. Kevin, another student, joins us. We gather in a small room in the back of the restaurant and squeeze around a large, round table. The heat in the room is oppressive, with just a fan in the corner to blow around the thick, humid air. Bugs are stuck in spider webs in the upper corners of the room, and the floor is coated with waxy grime. I settle into my chair, my stomach ill-prepared for another meal of unidentifiable food. Ever

MELISSA GRUNOW

since the night I threw up the burnt, plastic-smelling beef, my tolerance for Chinese food has dropped more each day. I'm losing anywhere from five to ten pounds a week, completely lacking appetite.

All the dishes are placed in the center on a lazy Susan that we rotate, picking at the food with our chopsticks or spooning concoctions into our own tiny bowls. Various seafood dishes are placed in front of us, their shells or scales and eyes still intact. I look over at Nikki, and she knows I'm going to struggle to eat. I pick up what I later learn to be a pig intestine with my chopsticks, set it on my plate, and poke at it while I flash an awkward smile around the table, hoping they don't notice that I'm not eating. Each time I sit down to an unfamiliar meal, I remember Nikki's duck head from the first day in the cafeteria, and I regret my snarky remarks. Beyond that first day, she has had no trouble with the food. I am not so fortunate.

Another dish is placed on the Susan and Nikki elbows me. "Look," she says with excitement in her voice. It's scrambled eggs and tomatoes. I relax a little and exhale. Scrambled eggs and tomatoes was the most familiar food I had eaten since coming to China, and it hadn't let me down yet.

I spin the Susan around and position the bowl in front of me. I pick up the big serving spoon and scoop all the way to the bottom, only to bring a whole fish the size of a large minnow to the surface. I let out a startled yelp, and drop the spoon back into the bowl.

"Oh, the fish! Watch out!" Billie says.

I sit back in my seat. No eggs and tomatoes for me. I feel like I should be starving, but the intense heat and humidity prevent me from feeling hunger.

Dick's uncle rotates the Susan so the egg dish is in front of him and scoops the fish into his bowl. He pops the whole thing into his mouth, chewing through bones and scales and eyes, crunching happily from across the table.

I pick up the glass in front of me and sip my tea, the loose leaves tickling my lips. It will be another night of eating from the peanut butter jar that I smuggled over in my suitcase.

After dinner, we walk along a quiet road through a bamboo forest, the shoots as thick as baseball bats, shoots that tower over us and block the setting sun. The bugs are quiet, leaving us alone for once, and the humidity subsides a little. We come upon a stream and Dick's mom stands on the bank and points out orange carp flipping their fins among the rocks. We continue along the road, Dick and Kevin chase each other in spurts, Nikki and I trailing behind them. I call them over and we line up and link arms. I show them how to walk in unison as I sing, "Hey! Hey! We're the Monkees!" their laughter drowning out my voice. Dick and Kevin skip a few steps, then connect their arms to walk like The Monkees again, their skinny legs crossing over in front of them as they climb the road ahead.

At night in the hotel, Nikki's first instinct is to turn on the television, even though there are only three channels and none of them are in English. Occasionally, we have access to BBC and one day we had an hour of music videos on MTV before the screen went blue. The television becomes background noise while we attempt to journal or unwind, but we always end up talking.

I learn that Nikki's guy back home isn't very considerate or respectful, and she hasn't made any effort to e-mail or otherwise contact him as a result of her realization.

Their mutual friends all tell her about his behavior with other women when she's not around, but she can't bring herself to end it.

MELISSA GRUNOW

"Why not?"

She shrugs, and I believe that she really doesn't know.

I don't know, either. I don't have advice for her. I had been dating my boyfriend for about nine months and couldn't get over the idea that he was just a little too comfortable and accepting of my month-long absence.

On our first day off, our chaperones take us by bus to Hangzhou, a city so beautiful and so rich in trade that Italian explorer Marco Polo called it the "City of Heaven" when he traveled to China during the Yuan Dynasty. He was the first Western visitor to the city, and is recognized with a statue of his likeness erected near West Lake.

Our group is made up of the eight of us Americans and our Chinese tour guides. When we arrive in Hangzhou, they warn us against pickpockets. "Many people. Hold your bag." We climb off the bus and walk toward West Lake for a boat tour. School-age children crowd around us. They're around the same age as our students and also know a little English.

A small girl walks right up to me and stares at my face until I look down at her. "Are you from America?" she asks me.

I kneel down so I am eye level with her. "Yes I am. What is your name?"

She giggles, suddenly shy that I'm paying her attention. She mutters a name that I can't understand, but I smile anyway. Around her, a small group of her classmates look on and nudge closer to watch our interaction.

I dig into the bottom of my bag and pull out a pencil with my university's logo on it. I study it for a second and hand it to the girl in front of me. She takes it in her hand and stares at it intently, her eyes large and focused. Her friends squirm in and push each other to get a look at the gift. They flash me their best grins and offer me greetings, not knowing much more English. I hold out my empty hand and shrug. I have nothing left to offer them.

The sun climbs higher in the sky, and the day heats up just like the others as July is the hottest month of the year, and also the most humid. There is no shade to hide under, no air-conditioned buildings to gather in. We stand to the side while our guides get us tickets for the boat ride. The Chinese are walking around with umbrellas to block the sun or cover themselves with long sleeves to shield their pale skin, whereas we welcome the direct light that darkens our hues.

I look up and see a small group of men slyly taking our picture with their camera phones, acting casual and nonchalant. I flash them a peace sign and a smile, and within minutes the crowd of onlookers has grown exponentially. Some come up and wiggle their way into our group to smile as a friend takes their picture with us foreigners. A man squeezes in next to me and grins into the crowd and at a camera. After his photo is taken, he turns to me, runs his hand down my long, curly red hair and says, "Beautiful."

I cringe a little and step away as I realize the size of the crowd. We're practically surrounded by Chinese paparazzi who don't hesitate to get close and touch us as though we're goats at a petting zoo.

I turn to Nikki. "We're never going to be able to get out of here."

She nods. "This is scary."

The mob circles even tighter around us.

I reach down and clutch my bag, and I can feel my wallet still settled in the bottom. I'm slightly relieved, though the fact that I haven't been robbed yet doesn't take away from the fear of the impending throng.

MELISSA GRUNOW

Our guide breaks through the crowd, waves her hand over her head and yells, "Follow me," as she turns and walks toward the lake. And just like that, the gawkers disperse.

On West Lake, I slump into a seat, overwhelmed by a humidity that's inescapable. I start to feel dizzy. A native of Michigan, I spent my life growing up around water. I am underwhelmed by a lap around a lake on a boat. I reach up to push my hair away from my face. There's no place to go to hide from the sun or the stares, so I turn toward the water, close my eyes, and plead for the ride to end.

When the boat docks, I step off and quickly find a bench where I can sit down. Our guide is soon prodding us up a path until we reach a large concrete area, flanked by small souvenir shops. I look up, and see a mountain of stairs leading up Sunset Hill to the Leifeng Pagoda, a five-story tall tower with eight sides. Leifeng was originally built in 977, attacked by the Japanese in 1924, and rebuilt with modern amenities (including an escalator and air-conditioning) in 2002.

Despite the heat, I decide to take the stairs to the top, cutting over to the escalator about halfway, unable to make it to the base of the pagoda on my own. I throw a coin into the ruins of the previous tower that are on display once we get inside, as it's supposed to bring good luck. I climb and climb and make it to the top floor to marvel at the famous ornamented ceiling. I walk around with my chin tilted upward, and bump into a toddler who is wearing nothing more than loose-fitting pants that are split at the crotch.

I mumble apologies that nobody hears and wouldn't understand anyway, and go back to taking pictures before I rest on a bench along the outer wall. The same child that I bumped into squats down and pees on the floor of the Leifeng Pagoda, just underneath the solid copper, hand-molded ceiling. His parents praise him, and I raise my eyebrows and stare, not believing what I'm seeing. I look around for Nikki, but she is out on the observation balcony and the rest of the group has split up throughout the pagoda, so I'm left to witness this defilement of a public monument on my own.

I get up and walk outside to where Nikki is taking pictures of West Lake from the balcony. Ramiz is chatting her up, trying to find some way to get her to notice him.

I start to tell them what I just saw, but it's a story I want to save for Nikki, so instead I say, "I can't believe how hot it is. This is unreal."

"I know," Ramiz says. "I've never had upper foot sweat before. That's new." He flashes Nikki a smile to see if she finds his joke funny, but she is studying the images on her camera.

I lean against the railing and slump a little. I've seen too much. I want to go back to Changxing, to the comfort of the compound, and the familiarity of my classroom, to the smiles of my students. My version of China is one of body-obsessed, xenophobic, pushy, hurried people without concern for public manners and personal space. However, my experience in the Chinese classroom is a place of inspiration, of seeing excitement in children who are shy at first, but then loving, giving, and craving the opportunity to learn, no matter their initial skill level.

A week later is our last day in the classroom at Changxing. Instead of teaching our scheduled lesson plans, we turn on music at full volume in all four classrooms, and do a Conga line throughout the school. Ramiz and Courtney lead a group of students in the "YMCA" and Leslie does an interview in English for a local television show. The kids are running around tossing balloons in the air and wearing party hats, as we made some attempt to teach them about birthdays and holidays that morning. While hanging paper chains throughout the room, I give the kids instructions; many ignore me and continue to color their pictures that they will then tape to the cinderblock walls.

"Ugh," I turn to Nikki, "why aren't they *listening*?" Dick looks over at me when he hears "listen," a look of recognition on his face. Most of the others continue working on their projects, happily chatting to each other in Mandarin. I realize then that while they may be listening, they can't understand me. That's when it hits me that I've been working with a group of non-native English speakers for two weeks, and became so accustomed to our routine that I forgot that we don't speak the same language.

That night we go out with Billie and Vivian who wander into a little shop and instruct us to wait on the sidewalk. They come out and take us to a tea house where they hand us each a gift: a personalized rubber stamp with our names in Chinese characters and English letters.

We are to leave for Huzhou in the morning and start teaching at Huzhou #4 Middle School the day after. On our last night in Changxing where we don't quite feel like foreigners anymore, where we have a sense of belonging, a sense of connection with Billie and Vivian, I use my rubber stamp on a tea house napkin, leaving my mark in Changxing, a foreigner in a foreign city who feels like she's leaving home in the morning.

FIRE AND WATER

"Deep into that darkness peering, long I stood there,
wondering, fearing, doubting, dreaming dreams
no mortal ever dared to dream before."
—EDGAR ALLAN POE, "THE RAVEN"

One day it started to rain, and for the rest of that day, it didn't stop. Instead, the water falling from the sky picked up velocity and filled the streets the way a faucet fills a bathtub. The freeway flooded until the water level reached the overpass. Stalled cars were abandoned after their passengers wriggled out through open windows and swam to the surface. It was nearly midnight before the water level receded enough for me to leave the elevated parking lot where I was stranded for three hours with a front-row seat to what I was sure was the end of the world.

I could see the two-foot water line etched into the basement drywall from the open door on the side of the house. I scrambled down the stairs and stood among the ruins. Not only was everything saturated, the water had risen so fast that it picked up objects and scattered them. The furnace short-circuited. The pilot light on the hot water tank extinguished. My cats cried in confusion as they cowered atop plastic storage bins, the photo albums, yearbooks, and other keepsakes inside irreparably damaged. It would take days to dig out and fill the curb with destroyed belongings, to rip out carpeting, to sort through what could be salvaged, which was very little.

It was a week before the local stations covered the storm, and only then because of the complaints from neighborhoods about delayed trash pick-up, the overwhelming stench of rot along the streets and the vermin that scavenged them. It would be weeks before the insurance company determined it had no obligation to cover the damage because I didn't have flood insurance. It would be months before the drywall was ripped out and covered with rot-resistant wainscoting, the concrete floor disinfected, sanded, and painted, the mold spores hopefully eradicated. Only then did the president declare the flood a national emergency. The damage, hospitalizations, death tolls, the sewage that filled the streets and basements of Detroit, none of it had made national news until desperate homeowners reached out to FEMA for some kind of reprieve.

"A flood is worse than a fire. After a flood, you'll worry whenever it rains," he said.

Whenever it rains. In Michigan, it rains half the year. Then there are the months of snow that piles up and melts, but has nowhere to go when the ground is frozen. When it's not raining, the sun beats down through a haze of humidity that singes the landscaping, turns the grass brown, and skin sticks to itself and everything it touches. I long for the cold, wet days of fall and early spring, but they are momentary. The weather is unpredictable and inconsistent. It's often moody and violent, and when the sky cracks open, nothing—nobody—is safe. Afterward, I walked the perimeter of my house looking for areas that water could puddle during rainstorms. It didn't matter that the water had actually risen up through the drain pipes in the basement floor because of a failed city sewer system, underground aqueducts with missing copper pipes that had been stolen and sold for scrap. At night, thunder jolted me awake anyway, and I listened to the rain against the roof, scratching at the windows, always anticipating another invasive act of God.

The remains of a fire will loiter: the ash and soot coating everything in its path as it spreads for miles, depending on weather and wind speed; the charred remains of the damaged structure seeps into the ground, damaging the soil. The smell burrows in so deeply that anything untouched by flames will be damaged anyway. The aftermath of a fire is infinite; water eventually recedes, though recovery isn't a guarantee.

"At least with a fire, there's closure," he continued.

I nodded, though I didn't agree. I didn't want to get into a discussion with this coworker in which we ranked from bad to awful the severities of loss and suffering. I didn't need closure. I just wanted to go home and clean out my basement.

There are two things that I do with wood: either cut it and assemble it into something purposeful or burn it. In the dark, discarded wood catches heat in a fire pit on the corner of my backyard patio. As the flames die down, I toss in cardboard boxes, unwanted circulars, and junk mail. There is more smoke than fire, though I don't bother to change seats or adjust the smoldering stack. My mind jolts to the album of wedding photos in my living room, and I wonder what it would look like to watch the protective plastic melt through the prints. What would become of the gilded gold and lace dress hanging in the back of my closet? How much smoke would there be if I tossed it all onto the fire? Would it give me closure to destroy these few remaining relics of an identity that never had a chance to fully take shape?

I don't bother to brush away the sawdust that collects on my clothes, in my hair. It sticks to my forehead, shiny with sweat; it frames my face when I remove the goggles to check my measurements and prepare for another cut. The drone of the jigsaw overcomes the distant noises of children in the neighborhood, the kicking on of sprinklers, the guttural wail of Harley engines. Vice grips hold the pine planks in place as the vibrations reverberate through my hands. A strand of hair falls loose from my ponytail, a futile obstruction that should break my concentration, but it doesn't.

I build so that I have less to lose. I build so I have something leftover to burn.

In elementary school, we had assemblies about fire safety. They warned us about playing with matches, letting Christmas trees dry out, leaving candles burning unattended. Local fire-fighters demonstrated their oxygen tanks and passed around their hats for us to touch and tap with our knuckles. Smoky the Bear became a cultural icon, warning each and every one of us, "Only *you* can prevent forest fires." I went camping with my Girl Scout troop exactly once, but it was enough to remember a detailed lesson on how to put out a campfire and check for hidden embers lurking beneath the ash, just waiting for a gust of wind to release them into the surrounding woods littered with dried pine needles.

I didn't become familiar with the concept of controlled burns until I learned about the Kirtland's warbler, an endangered Michigan bird native of jack pine forests. They make their nests on the ground, but will only do so if the pines are young, between 6 and 22 years old, and between 5 and 20 feet tall, when the lowest branches are closest to the ground. These low branches begin to die after the tree is 15 years old; the higher the jack pine grows, the higher, too, become its lowest branches.

Jack pines repopulate when their cones are heated from fire and seeds are released. In an effort to rejuvenate the

Kirtland's warbler population, the U.S. Forest Service conduct controlled burns to rid the area of old jack pines and release the seeds to grow new ones.

In other words, we burn trees so others can grow. We destroy jack pines so birds can live. South American farmers burn the rain forest to clear land for their crops. In sub-Saharan Africa, fields are even burned as a mechanism to herd livestock.

I burn leftover scraps from my woodshed to make room for new projects. We burn chopped wood in metal pits to stay warm while camping and to have something to stare into while we share stories and drink beer. We burn to live, we burn for a songbird to survive, we burn when we think we can control it, but we use a cartoon bear to teach children to be afraid of it.

When I was four, my family moved from an apartment in Saginaw to a trailer park in Belleville. A neighbor girl who would soon become my best friend hovered at the edge of the neighbor's driveway. I waved from the front door, but she wouldn't come closer. She was too scared to because the last home that sat on our lot had burned to the ground.

Six years later, my parents were divorced, and my mother lived in a second-floor apartment of a house in Dearborn. My brother and the boy who lived in the first-floor apartment had gotten their hands on fireworks and were lighting them in the large, unkempt backyard, laughing maniacally as each one exploded into the air. Even though my brother was younger than me, the neighbor boy was older, so I sat on the back porch and watched them, eager he would notice me. He said nothing, but I thought I saw him glance my way a few times, and that was enough to keep me from going back inside.

My brother held what looked like a foam replica of a Wright Brothers airplane away from him with one hand and lit the wick with the other. The wings fluttered as the wick burned down, and he tossed it into the air. It flew upward and then changed direction until it was flying right at me. I turned my head just in time for the rocket to singe my hair, instead of my face.

"Don't tell Mom," my brother begged. "Don't tell *Dad*."

This was two years after the 1988 summer drought, the hottest and driest in Southeastern Michigan since the 1930s. That year, homeowners were fined if their families used too much water. Lawns turned from green to brown to dust under the relentless sun. Forests caught fire and disintegrated to ash. Water levels sank to surprising lows and irrigation become impossible. Farms couldn't harvest their crops. Livestock died. Food costs skyrocketed. The drought spread to thirty percent of the country and lasted throughout the mid-1980s. In total, the lack of rain and the endless high temperatures racked up $39 billion in loss; it had been the costliest in U.S. history of any natural disaster that had come before.

Nearly twenty years later, Hurricane Katrina produced such strong storms and sudden rainfall in New Orleans that the levees were breached. Foundations eroded, embankments were compromised, and eventually the flood-protection system failed altogether as water rushed over and washed away the levees and eighty percent of the city along with them.

There have been other natural disasters: snowfall so fast and so heavy that people had to climb on top of their houses and shovel their roofs for fear the weight of the accumulation would cause them to collapse. Earthquakes destroyed bridges in the faraway land of California.

When natural disasters force people to evacuate their homes and entire cities are swallowed by water or shredded by wind storms, local authorities encourage the residents to write their social security numbers on their forearms so their bodies can be identified if they don't make it out alive.

Tornadoes tore apart homes and families and terrified me as a child. We had tornado drills in school where we had to file into the hallway, sit on the floor facing the wall, and tuck our heads into our chests.

One August in particular, everything around us went so quiet we could almost hear the air getting thicker just before the rains came, followed by the imminent threats of tornado warnings that flashed across the bottom of the television screen. After we changed into pajamas, my brother and I sat on the floor in the living room and tried to ignore the snowy picture that the antenna just couldn't fix. He nudged me every time the map of our part of the state changed color and asked me if that meant the tornado was coming for us next. Outside, the wind blew harder as the sky got darker; it got under the siding of our trailer and howled throughout the living room. Lights flickered. The tree in our yard shook. Then the rain fell harder and harder, and we listened for any sign that it was getting worse, until we had to go to bed.

There were many nights that year when my mother woke us up and made us hunker down in the hallway because it was the only space in our trailer that didn't have a window. I coached my three-year-old brother on what to do from the tornado drills I had practiced in school. *Face the wall. Knees tucked in and head tucked under.* This was to protect us from flying shards of glass and other bits of destruction. *Don't talk.* I never fully understood how silence was going to protect us, but we shut up anyway.

We brought our pillows and blankets into the hallway, sat on the floor and stared at each other, our eyes wide, our mouths closed, and our ears tuned in to the wind crashing up against the side of our trailer, howling, howling, the sky too dark to warn us if the tornado was on its way.

I knew that if a tornado actually hit our area, all the hunkering and wishful thinking we could muster wouldn't stop the winds from picking up our entire aluminum home off its concrete foundation and chucking it into oblivion. Our screams, no doubt, would be lost in the roar of the storm.

Shortly after I was old enough to ride my bike throughout the trailer park without landmark boundaries—not that I had ever obeyed them anyway—my parents put me in charge of cruising around to look for the sheets of skirting that we had lost during the storm. Mobile homes sit about two or three feet above the ground to make space for water pipes underneath. Skirting is used to keep out animals and trash, and to make the trailer look less like a transient home.

The skirting were large slabs of metal that matched the siding of the trailer. Their edges were sharp, and the corners usually left me with scratches. They slid on a track underneath the house, and when it got windy enough, the edges would be caught just right and they would pull away, collecting with tree limbs, discarded toys, and other debris. The morning after bad storms, my friends and I would get on our bikes and pedal around the neighborhood looking for slabs of skirting that had blown off our house. They were heavy, big and awkward and we could usually only balance one at a time on our handlebars, and even then it was wobbly and slow-going. There were usually quite a few neighbors out looking for their own skirting, and sometimes we brought back slabs that didn't belong to us, sometimes someone else took our slab when it didn't belong to them.

I'd aim my bike tire at the worms that had stretched themselves long and skinny across the sidewalk and run them over. I'd feel especially pleased if my tire severed them, as if it were some kind of retribution for the gashes on my hands from the skirting's sharp edges. Anything, everything, can cut something else.

I learned how to grow grass from my father. Rake the area with a hoe, sprinkle the seed, and then cover it with peat moss. The moss keeps the ground damp and helps prevent birds and critters from eating the seeds before they take root. This process should be done every spring when the almost daily rain will keep the seeds watered and the ground soft and rich in nutrients for them to grow.

New grass isn't the only sign of life in the spring. Birds return to hover around the feeders I have hanging in the yard. The feeders tend to also attract squirrels, chipmunks, and even rats and raccoons, among other unwanted vermin. An online forum made up of neighbors living in my town discourage bird feeders for this reason, but I put the seeds out anyway, letting my dog out often to chase away the unwanted.

The year my dog killed a baby skunk in the backyard, the overwhelming smell of singed hair and burnt flesh filled my house quickly. I knew he had gotten into something, but it was too dark to know what for sure. Instead, I got him quickly into a bath and remained stumped that he continued to smell like a human incinerator no matter how much puppy shampoo I lathered into his body.

For two days, I left the carcass in the yard, a small lump of black and white fur barely visible from the window. I took the dog out on a leash and brought him back in as soon as he had done his business. I felt bad that the little critter never had a chance. I also felt disgusted by the smell and by the fact that I had to clean it up.

I finally sealed the body in a Ziploc bag, two shopping bags, and a heavy-duty trash bag before tossing it in the bin the day before trash collection. I took the hose and soaked the grass where the animal had died. I had no way of knowing for

MELISSA GRUNOW

sure that it would make any difference; all I knew was a dead baby skunk stank of burning flesh, and the only way I knew to combat the smell of fire was with water.

Perhaps the most epic story of fighting fire with water is in *Lysistrata*, an ancient Greek play. The men and women of Athens are at odds with each other as a war against Sparta rages in the background. The women want peace and their men to come home; the men insist that war is the only way to live. The women lock down the Acropolis and withhold sex until the war ends. Enraged, the men attempt to reclaim the Acropolis with fire, and the women respond by extinguishing the fire with water. The women have no political power, but they do have their sexuality and objects of domesticity—pitchers of water, lamps, spindles, and other items of the home—and they weaponize both in the name of peace.

When the two sides of sexual warfare are both women, the weapon is less obvious. At a gay bar in Phoenix—the very city named for the mythical bird that was reborn from ash—we gathered in the VIP section for Patti's birthday. The area was blocked off with a red velvet rope, the booths adorned in the same fabric. Against the flashing lights from the dance floor, our party room looked like it was on fire. Women danced on the bar in their underwear, their loose butts and flabby stomachs jiggling cellulite in time with the music.

"If I wanted to see that," Kelly said, "I would just look in the mirror." She laughed, and I looked away because her teeth bothered me.

"You'll like her," Patti had said before introducing us. "She's a redhead, like you, and my only other white girl friend. You're both afraid of the sun."

I met Patti while working for a small company when we both lived in New Mexico. All her friends were lesbian Latinas and a few gay men, and they took to calling me "White Girl" or "Straight Girl" as soon as they met me. I accepted the nicknames as terms of endearment, even though they kept me on the periphery of their tight-knit circle.

After Patti moved to Arizona and I moved back to Michigan, I flew out to Phoenix to celebrate her thirtieth birthday. It was there that I met Kelly, who was tall with straw-colored hair (*not* a redhead) and a cruel sense of humor. She liked to pinch Patti on the arms to see how hard she would have to press the skin together to make it bruise. In retaliation, Patti would slug her in the shoulder, but she never told Kelly to stop.

I didn't like Kelly. I especially didn't like that Patti liked Kelly. I wasn't entirely sure how Kelly felt about me, but she regarded me with suspicion. I was Patti's history and our loyalties ran deep because we had absolutely zero sexual attraction to one another.

Kelly, I presume, didn't buy it.

At the VIP table, Kelly picked up a lighter and ignited it, making the flame dance in the space between us. She turned it so the flame encircled the metal cover. "How hot do you think this needs to be before it will melt?" she asked. Before I could answer, she grabbed my hand and pushed the head of the lighter into my skin, just below my thumb knuckle.

"Kelly! What the fuck?" I yanked my hand away and plunked it down into a tumbler of ice water, the skin instantly turning an angry pink as heat radiated to my wrist.

She laughed, her mouth resembling the sucker end of a leech. She had branded me, marked me in such a way as if to announce to the world that I was not one of them.

The burn instantly bubbled into the shape of a horseshoe, a scar that took years to fade. Once it did, I became the rain in Phoenix. Non-existent.

In *Lysistrata*, the women are water, the men are fire. Each try to put the other out and both lose their molecular formula in the process. The women, however, do not have their common sense clouded by longing for bloodshed or crippling sexual desire. The play is revolutionary in that it presents women as the more sensible of the two sexes, a sharp contrast to contemporary belief that women are inferior because we are more emotional than logical, more erratic than focused. We fight these accusations by taking on roles traditionally assumed by men. We cut our own wood, build our own campfires, and clean up dead animals from the yard ourselves. We not only rip out the water damage before black mold can grow, we safeguard our houses against the next inevitable flood. We clean, construct, install, discard, rebuild, move forward. We eventually perceive two feet of water in our basements as an opportunity to start anew, rather than seeking the presumed closure that comes with a fire.

Closure is a drug of choice, an addiction that locks people into the conflicts of time and space. They are rats in a maze and hamsters running on a wheel. They are bitter, jealous lesbians in dark bars who scar people with lighters, and they are nervous little brothers who nearly maim their sisters with illegal fireworks. They are never satisfied until someone gives them permission to be satisfied. It's no way to live.

ECOSYSTEM

*"If ever there was a story without a shadow it would
be this: that we as women exist in direct sunlight only."*
—TERRY TEMPEST WILLIAMS, *WHEN WOMEN WERE BIRDS*

The first summer I lived in New Mexico, I was certain I would die there. The heat was ruthless and relentless, the sun mocking from on high every single moment I had ever cursed the cold, grey skies of Michigan winters. Everything once green yielded to triple-digit temperatures and surprising humidity. There was no going barefoot because the sidewalks were scalding. Yards had been dug out and turned into cactus gardens long before I arrived. I slept with icepacks tucked against my body and watched the skin around my eyes dry up and crack like clay. I cried in frustration that I had left behind the seasonal markers in Michigan. In autumn, the leaves didn't change color and shed from trees gradually. Instead, they crashed to the ground all at once in a collective suicide pact and turned brown within a day. The grass wasn't greener there; it was dead.

Well into the first year of graduate school, I began waking up every night gasping as my body hurled forward, desperate for air. I was disoriented by the darkness, my panic, the heavy blankets that trapped my body against the mattress.

My breathing croaked and fought against the neurons short-circuiting in my mind as I pushed away the covers and

MELISSA GRUNOW

turned until my feet were on the floor, my elbows on my knees. My husband woke, startled by my display, his arms flailing and fists pummeling into my back.

"What is *wrong* with you?" he grumbled. "What are you *doing*?"

If I told myself I needed to sleep or I would die, I would lie awake and wonder, *Is this when you will take me? I have so much work to do before I go.*

My backyard is full of sparrows. They are tiny, feisty little things whose wings flutter in rapid desperation as they hover and search for a safe landing spot on one of the many hanging feeders. Some take their chances with the discards that have fallen into the grass, hunting and pecking at the ground for a morsel. Trolling among them is an American crow, a few pigeons, maybe some robins, and—on rare days—a cardinal with a majestic crest atop his head.

In the spring, sparrows squawk and glare at each other, bickering like toddlers while my black cat watches with quiet stealth from an armchair. I tell people I put the feeders there for him, to give him something to look at during the day, but I spend almost as much time staring out the window as he does.

Blue jays will appear in the summer, though they've been less frequent since one got stuck and panicked while the others flew away. With gloved hands, I freed its head from the feeder's outer cage. Off he flew with gratitude in his wingspan.

My grandpa was a bird watcher and kept logs of his sightings. If I woke up early enough in the summer, I would join him on his neighborhood walks, where he would talk to me about the birds, the squirrels, the many changes Saginaw had gone through since he was a boy. He pointed out houses that he helped his father build. There was even a street a few blocks away from where he had always lived with my grandma that bore his family name—Bock—that was changed from Baak when his family immigrated from Germany to make it easier to pronounce in America.

When I was young, I wondered how it was that he knew so much about everything, how he could rewire toasters to make them last longer, how his garage was filled with every tool and gadget imaginable, how he fixed anything and everything that broke, rather than replacing it.

Now if I'm awake early enough, I'll see a black squirrel scurry down the roof of the garage, swat at the cages, hoping to rattle something loose, hoping to have his fill before the back door opens and the dog chases him away.

Duke never catches the squirrels. He never catches the rabbits, either, the two who must have been born in a yard nearby. They are partial to the weeds, wildflowers, and clover that grow naturally along my property line. When spring began, there was just one rabbit, small but independent, that huddled in the hostas and ran for the opening under the fence when chased by the dog. After a few weeks, there were two rabbits that would give chase, one bolting to the left and circling the garage, the other and more experienced of the two making his escape through the space behind the lilies. I wondered if maybe Duke liked the chase more than the possibility of catching the rabbits, for I was certain that he had come close enough so many times that he could have, but he never opened his mouth, never prepared his jaw to receive them.

I have watched Duke leap from the ground and snap at the sparrows and succeed in trapping them in his jaw. Almost immediately, though, he drops them to the ground and seems surprised to find that they are no longer moving, that their little bones and little bodies were no match for his strength. I

MELISSA GRUNOW

don't know if he realizes that he has killed them or if he even knows what that means. He doesn't tear into their bodies or take pride in the kill by bringing me the carcass. Instead, he drops them, looks around for others that are flying, and circles the yard as they synchronize and swoop away until he's back in the house and they can safely return to the bird feeders.

—

In the nineteenth century, it was standard practice among the middle class to take post-mortem photos to memorialize the dead. The adults were propped up in chairs and often surrounded with flowers; children in their cribs were posed with their favorite toy. Because child mortality rates were so high, post-mortem photos were often the only photos family had of children who died in infancy.

—

It's become a routine for me to sit on the steps when I let Duke outside, especially in the early morning after we've just woken up and before I begin my day. It's a comfort to both of us to have these few minutes together in the dark, dew heavy on the grass, the city quiet around us. I'm awake before any of my neighbors, before most people have begun their morning commute, so even the whirring of the traffic from the nearby freeway is subdued. Rarely do I need to call him to the door in the morning. Instead, he hears the release of the latch, and I listen for the click of his nails on the hardwood floor. I slip into whatever pair of shoes are available, and he slips outside past me, down the steps and stands at attention in the yard, sniffing the air, and scanning the grass for movement for any nocturnal creatures still lingering from the night before.

For the past few weeks, I've been on alert as well, catching glimpses of a rat creeping in the shadows along the side of the garage, scavenging for birdseed littering the ground or rotting apples that have dropped from the neighbor's tree and into my yard. I wonder if it's the same rat or if there are many that are taking turns spreading their pestilence. The online forums for my city are filled with posts from neighbors commenting about the rat problem, pointing fingers at possible causes: the nearby zoo, the many restaurants and dumpsters down-town, pet owners who don't clean up dog waste, unsecured trash cans, backyard gardens, compost containers, and—of course—bird feeders. There are pleas to not put out rat poison as it has killed pets, opossums (a rat's natural enemy), and raccoons. I have rid my yard of every type of rat attraction except for the birdseed because I like to watch the birds flutter and gather around the food from the window in my home office. Although there are mostly sparrows—not robins as I would expect in Michigan—I'm thrilled to see the occasional cardinal, blue jay, finch, killdeer, and others that I have not yet learned to identify.

I don't chime in to the discussion in these online forums and defend the sanctity of my birdfeeders. Instead, I keep them hidden behind the planks of the privacy fence and watch from the window. In the summer, I'll sit in stillness on the patio and the bravest will gather on the feeders across the yard. I listen to their song, their squabbling chirps, and close my eyes in hopes I can learn to distinguish them by the sounds they make.

In the early morning, though, there are no birds. A shadow ambles behind the bushes lining the garage, and Duke chases it deep into the backyard into the darkness beyond the reach of the porch light. I'm more calm than usual during this chase, certain nothing will come of it as usual, annoyed with the rat that has ignored its eviction notice.

Paws rustle in the grass, and that's when I hear first the squeal and the jingling of Duke's tags. I don't need to see it to

MELISSA GRUNOW

know what's happened—he caught the rat and shook it hard. The squeal was the rat's death cry, distinctive from the dog's cry when he's hurt.

I call Duke back to me, and he comes to the porch immediately.

"Did you catch it?" I ask, even though I know he can't answer me.

Instead, he sits and his jaw slacks into a pant. A single drop of blood rolls down his incisor and drips onto the concrete slab between us.

When I return home after work, I find the rat's carcass with its neck snapped curled near the fence. *He almost made it,* I think before scooping his body into a trash bag with a shovel.

It's not the first dead rat I've had to clean up and toss into the trash, but it's the first one where I was witness to its death. Someone asked me afterward if I had taken a picture of it.

"Of course not," I said.

"I would have," was the reply. "Your dog is a hunter. That's something to commemorate."

~

I once attended a funeral on the arm of an ex-boyfriend when his aunt died in the hospital due to neglect. The family was outraged, deeply in mourning, and quite forthcoming with wailings and other outcries of emotion throughout the wake. Near the end of the visitation, the woman's niece, Jessica, wanted to take pictures of the many flower baskets and displays, as well as the casket because she picked out the quote, "I love turkey-lurkey," that was stitched into the fabric. She looked around nervously at the few family members and friends in their seats, afraid of what they would think, what reasons they could imagine that this young woman was photographing a dead body.

Jessica looked at me and shook her head. She couldn't do it. She slid her phone shut and reach toward her pocket to put it away.

I gently nudged her and held my hand out. I would take the pictures for her. If she wanted that memory, she should have it.

—

It's five o'clock in the morning in January, and I'm digging a hole behind the garage in the dark. It's cold, but not as cold as it should be this time of year. Luckily, the ground isn't frozen or covered in snow anymore. Instead, it's been raining for the past week, softening and warming the soil enough for me to pierce the earth and dig.

I'm crying, and the hole is even more difficult to see through my tears. My arms wobble under the weight of the dirt that I'm attempting to cast aside. I hit a tree root a few inches down, and it catches the spade, dropping dirt back into the hole.

I drag the back of my hand across my forehead to brush the hair away from my sweaty face and sigh. For a yard that has no trees, there are certainly a lot of roots to contend with.

I finally toss the shovel aside and stomp back into the garage. Not for a lantern, but for branch trimmer that resembles bolt cutters and feels just as heavy. I cut the root and pry it out so I can keep digging.

I need to hurry. I'll be late for work if I don't get into the shower by six o'clock. I've only been at this job for about a month, and I can't be late. Maybe the water will calm me and stop the tears as it washes away the dirt.

I realize I have no idea how big or how deep to make this hole.

She died lying on her side, her legs outstretched in front of her, paws crossed one over the other. I hoped she was sleeping, but I knew she wasn't. I knew it before I said her name,

MELISSA GRUNOW

before I knelt down to shake her a little, then pet her. I picked her up to cuddle her one last time, but her body had already gone into rigor, leaving me with no easy way to hold her. I laid her on the foot of my bed and wrapped her in a towel before taking her downstairs and into the backyard, gazing into the darkness and wondering where—how—I was going to bury my fifteen-year-old cat, who in her final moments and with her last remaining energy, jumped down off the bed where I slept, and let go of the life she had been hanging onto all week.

In Mexico, they celebrate *Dia de los Muertos*, or Day of the Dead, during the two days following Halloween. This holiday—much like the post-mortem photos of the Victorian era—are for the respect and remembrance of the dead. Families build private altars for those who have passed on and decorate them with flowers, the deceased's possessions, and gifts for the departed, including *Calaveras*, skulls shaped from sugar.

In Middle America, we distance ourselves from the dead. After funerals, we put our people in the ground or in urns, and come to terms with their passing individually and privately. There is no annual reuniting with our loved ones. Often, it's not even acceptable to name the dead in conversation out of fear of bringing to the surface the feelings of sadness and loss.

Las Calaveras Catrinas are among the most popular figures in celebrating the Day of the Dead. The term itself translates to both "dapper skeleton" and "elegant skull," and they act as symbols of how Latin cultures think of the death as co-existing with life.

I see the feathers before I realize that they are still attached to the rotting corpses of dead seagulls stuck in the grates of the Rouge Bridge, a traffic artery that connects two sides of Jefferson Avenue. Hundreds have died, and those that are still alive circle the sky and swoop down toward the cars like suicide bombers. Others cannibalize remains of the deceased, flying away at the last possible second to avoid becoming roadkill themselves. The land surrounding the bridge, owned by the Great Lakes Water Authority, is where the birds have chosen to nest, produce offspring, and soon die in the streets. The white birds contrast sharply against the black smokestacks emitting flames and pollution on nearby Zug Island. The island is inhabited only by the steel mill that has closed down local businesses and chased away residents of nearby Delrey. The few who remain are plagued with respiratory infections from the plant and the frequent arson fires set to abandoned buildings.

Local media outlets have given little press coverage to the dead seagulls, beyond heavily photographing and lightly speculating on the cause of the issue. The Department of Natural Resources recently got involved to test a sampling of the carcasses, linking their death to dehydration and impact from the passing cars. Although the DNR has claimed they don't pose an environmental threat, the autopsies have shown signs of high population-level stress, including edema in the lungs and lesions, their bodies clearly diseased. There are more than 300 dead seagulls, many of them still Teds at less than a year old. This is surprising, considering seagulls are protective of their young—the little ones normally don't leave their nests until they are able to fly and find their own food. However, many of the dead gulls on the Rouge Bridge were too young to fly, and it's believed they were hit by cars while walking along the grates alone in search of food.

I am convinced that if there was ever a zombie apocalypse, Zug Island would be ground zero. The high-security facility of manufacturing secrets, the dead seagulls, the nearby vacant homes and charred buildings have turned this area of Southwest Detroit into a post-apocalyptic dystopia. Although seagulls are protected by wildlife conservation laws that prevent humans from shooting them or destroying their nests, there has been no effort to save them from the fate they have created by making the treatment plant their home.

~

I didn't die in New Mexico, though it was not futile of me to fear it. It was Sean who died. A third-year poetry student in the MFA program, he lived in an apartment with a leaking roof, and the monsoon rains in August filled the plaster walls of his bedroom until they crawled with black mold. He started sleeping on his couch during the day and he wrote poems on a typewriter well into the night.

> *Sometimes I don't know*
> *where this dirty road has taken me.*
> Then I remember: the gas station,
> the post office parking lot with the onion patch adjacent;
> there you can cry for everything openly & everyone is fine
> with it; assuming you just got there
> hoping you're about to leave.[1]

He had been sick for at least a week, struggling to breathe and his skin pale. When he didn't show up for his Monday night workshop, a classmate drove to his home, entered through the side door that was always unlocked, and found him five days dead on his living room floor. She rifled through his address book to find his mom's number and fed his cat before stepping back outside to call the police.

---

[1] Excerpt from "The Accountants Elegy for Praise" by Sean Branson

Sean used to say that he was surprised he had lived as long as he did. He was twenty-six.

I didn't understand until years later that what was happening to me when I woke up at night heaving and shuddering was a series of panic attacks. Eventually they stopped and were replaced by dreams of loss and death, dreams where I shape-shifted into animals that could run away, fly away, away from the situation I felt stuck in during my waking life.

It wasn't just the pressures of graduate school or teaching college-level classes of freshmen students when I was just twenty-one. Rather, it was the sprawling scarcity of the desert, the traffic congested onto roads that had been determined long ago by cattle grazing patterns, making it difficult for me to navigate my way around town for more than a year. It was the heat, the perpetual fringes of dehydration, and the small apartment I shared with a man who was a tyrannical overlord of our life together, squeezing freedom out of me and taking it for himself. I would have left him sooner had Sean not died, but the death of our peer forced me to cling to any representation of life I could endure. It was a ruthless pursuit for vitality until I became strong enough to leave the nest and fly.

MELISSA GRUNOW

PART 3
SUPPRESSED

BITE

"I know I must conceal my sentiments: I must smother hope; I must remember that he cannot care much for me. For when I say that I am of his kind, I do not mean that I have his force to influence, and his spell to attract: I mean only that I have certain tastes and feelings in common with him. I must, then, repeat continually that we are forever sundered:—and yet, while I breathe and think, I must love him."
—CHARLOTTE BRONTË, *JANE EYRE*

We were in a hotel the first time I went down on him. He apologized as I descended his body—grazing my lips and tongue over his chest, stomach, hips—that he might not be able to get off that way, that he never could before. I took his admittance as a personal challenge. I wrapped my lips over my teeth to prevent them from scraping before taking him into my mouth. I was patient and giving, adding vibration by moaning through it along with him. His hands moved from my hair to my shoulders, finally resting on the back of my head. When he came, he gyrated against my face like a woodpecker burrowing into a tree trunk and then pulled me back by my hair so suddenly that I bit my tongue. I smiled instead of wincing. I had done something no one else could.

If we had gone to a restaurant on our first date instead of meeting for drinks and karaoke, I'm not sure there would have been a second date. The first thing I ever saw him eat was a burger stacked so tall with toppings that he had to stretch his mouth wide to get his teeth around it before biting down assertively, splattering beef juice, condiments, and bits of bleu cheese crumbles onto his plate, the table, his lap. His large tongue pushed the food around his mouth, and I watched it fold and masticate through the opening in his lips, like clothes agitating in a washing machine.

When we ate together, I tried to focus my attention on my own food or out the window or the screen of my cell phone. I would turn on the stereo in the background at home to drown out the noise of his aggressive chomping, the smack of his lips, the slurping of guzzled water out of pint glasses. His table manners embarrassed me.

After we separated, he would text me occasionally. *Want to grab a bite?*

No, I said, without explanation. Or I simply never replied.

Shortly after he moved out, I spent a weekend binge watching the *Twilight* movies. It wasn't for the love story or the dialogue, as both are trite and bewildering. It was for the power dynamics in the relationship. What struck me the most was how little biting occurs in the story, even though it's a series about vampires. When it does happen, biting is violence or biting is love and it seems love and violence are interchangeable. It's codependence in its sexiest form, and we eat it up. Even when it's ugly and awful and we know from the start that someone is going to end up devoured, we crave it. Why do we love the love stories where one person is inevitably destroyed for, or by, the other?

It's instinctual for all animals to bite. In defense, in play, in pleasure, even for comfort. When I pet my cat, he purrs and shifts, inching toward me. If my hand spends too much time on his belly or even dares to tug at his paws, he bites. If he gets too comfortable, too relaxed, too happy, he bites. He wriggles his all-black body into corners and sprawls upside down, baring his bottom teeth. *Bat cat*, I call him.

Before we were married, I hosted Easter dinner at my house for my parents, his parents, and my sister's family. The gathering took me a week to prepare. I scrubbed the house, raked out flowerbeds and spread mulch around annuals just beginning to sprout up from the dirt. I bought new placemats, additional silverware, serving platters, a gravy boat. I had to call my mom to ask how to pick out a ham from the meat case at the supermarket as I had never made one before. I served mashed potatoes instead of the cheesy hash browns his mom was known for along with asparagus and Brussels sprouts as they were my favorite vegetables. My niece filled glasses with ice and water and nobody seemed happy with where they were seated at the dining table, though they emptied the serving plates, clinking forks against knives before devouring the food. I watched him slide remains onto his fork with his thumb before licking it clean, and I hoped my parents didn't notice. I glared at him when he tilted his chair back and balanced on two hind legs while telling yet another story about work. The dinner rolls were nearly black on the bottom because I forgot they were in the oven. I served them anyway.

I had to run the dishwasher before I could serve dessert because we ran out of forks. I served lemon squares and cheesecake pumpkin pie that his mother baked, accompanied by torn-off sheets of paper towel. "Don't you have any real napkins?" my mother asked. I did. They were cloth, bleached white, and sitting in the base of the washing machine because we had used them at dinner. "These are so *expensive* to just use as napkins," she remarked of the paper towels.

When everyone left, he and I sat together in silence on the patio and sipped beer straight from the bottle. He left the sliding door ajar for the dog and to eliminate one extra step impeding access to a second, and finally a third, round of drinks. As the sun settled behind the trees still leafless from a long winter, I crawled into bed exhausted.

Just as I was falling asleep, the dog started barking in the living room and wouldn't stop. It alarmed both of us because he never barked.

"You go," I said, and rolled over before closing my eyes.

I heard him descend the stairs. I heard the door close behind him and then his body crash into the door as he yelled, "Oh shit!"

Whatever it is, I thought. *He can deal with it*. After all, I had handled all of the dinner preparations and the cleaning up afterward.

"There's a bird in the house!" he yelled up the stairs.

I opened my eyes and knew immediately it wasn't a bird.

I found him and the dog hunched in the kitchen and watched a dark shadow circle the coved ceilings of the living room.

"It's a bat," I said. "Not a bird. A bat."

After letting the dog into the backyard, I went out the side door and propped open the front door from the outside while the bat hung upside down in the corner of the room. Maybe if it sensed the darkness, felt the cool night air wafting inside, he would find his way out. I opened the window and the screen, then turned on all the lights in the kitchen and dining room and the lamp in the corner of the living room.

"We need to get it out," I said as I worked while he stood there and watched the bat cautiously. "If it bites one of us, we're going to need rabies shots in the stomach."

Despite the light and the wide-open exits, the bat continued to circle the ceiling, then hang upside down again.

I retrieved a broom from the hall closet, while he retrieved his camera and started filming.

The bat returned to its spot in the corner and hung. I nudged it with the bristles of the broom and it started to fly again, lower this time, and headed straight for the camera.

He screamed. I swung the broom like I was trying to hit a homerun, made contact, and knocked the bat to the floor.

I was certain I'd killed it.

He continued to take pictures.

I had no idea how to dispose of a dead bat or if it was actually dead. I just needed to get it out of the house. I swept it outside, and as it careened into the night air, its wings spread and it flew away.

I turned to say something and found him already scrolling through the pictures on his camera. He didn't make a move to close the windows or the door. He didn't make an effort to turn out the lights. He just stood there, staring intently at his photos.

"Let the dog in, will you?" I asked. "I'm going to bed."

As a puppy, my dog would latch onto my hands and wrists with his mouth, as if to say, *Come with me*. His incisors would rarely puncture my skin, but I knew it was a habit he needed to break after he did the same to my three-old-niece and she shrieked, "He bited me!" as Gobstopper-sized tears rolled down her cheeks.

Now that he's older, I can stick my hand in his mouth without fear while he pants. I press my fingertips against the sharp points of his bottom teeth or grab claw-like until he pulls away, annoyed. Minutes later, I'll hear him in the next room chewing contentedly on a bone, propping it up between his front paws for a better angle. Nobody taught him he could hold onto it with something other than his mouth.

He greets people with the only language he knows. He'll lower his head and produce a long, howling growl—never a bark—until he gets a pat on the head or a greeting in return.

I don't notice it until someone new comes into the house, and I must explain away his behavior. "He won't bite," I reassure them. "He's just talking to you." Some nod but don't take their eyes off him, their skepticism apparent in the way they hover just inside the door. Others will reassure me with, *Oh, I love dogs!* or *I had a husky (or a German shepherd or a Labrador or a pit bull) growing up, so I get it,* and then they'll rustle his fur and ask to give him a treat.

I don't know if I ever went through that preschool phase of biting other kids. Estranged from my mother and the daughter of a man who doesn't talk about his life before his second marriage, I know very little about my childhood behaviors from others' stories. I don't remember any of my younger siblings as biters, either. When we fought, we would push, yell, and hit, but never bite. Biting wasn't something you did to get your toy back. Biting wasn't a way to win an argument. Biting wasn't how you established the sandbox, playground, or story circle as your domain. Biting was utilitarian, a way of consuming food, though never to share or exchange it.

At restaurants with his family, food was offered off each other's plates. "Wanna bite?" they would ask and offer a forkful of chicken, seafood, pasta. "Here, try this," they would say and pass their beverage around the table, each taking communal sips. I couldn't eat from another's fork or sip from another's cup and so I didn't partake in the banquet. Instead, I kept my eyes on my plate, my fork held firmly in my hand, and nibbled on the inside of my mouth, a habit that dentists have scolded me about for years. I did it to stay silent, to literally hold my tongue and prevent me from saying something that would probably be better left unsaid. For when I gave voice to my thoughts, the inevitable result was a raucous argument, the aftershocks of which would last for days.

We fought with fangs, words that bloodied and could not be swallowed. Together, we became animalistic, feral, desperate. I chewed my cheeks raw, felt them bleed and swell inside my lips. I devoured myself before he could. He didn't flirt with me anymore or call out, "Pretty girl!" when I came home from work. He barely looked up from his computer. "I'll give you space," he said, even though I didn't ask for it or want it. I wanted a version of him that he couldn't be. He wanted me to be happy, and I wasn't.

I'm not so sure it matters who did the biting first. It's not going to lead to deeper understanding about the erosion of our relationship. But if you must know, it was me, on our first date. The only table left at the karaoke bar was right next to the speaker. We stood close together to talk and when I leaned in to ask him to repeat his question, he kissed me. Softly at first, as if asking for permission. I moved my mouth to his ear to answer him and gripped his earlobe with my teeth. When he kissed me again, I locked onto his bottom lip. Not once do I remember him biting me. Not until the end.

I found a picture of them buried under some papers on his coffee table. In it, her eyes are closed tightly from laughing so hard. He has his mouth wide open, his teeth latched onto the curve of her cheekbone, looking directly into the camera. If I didn't know either of them, the picture would probably make me smile and think, *What a fun couple*. Instead, I was fraught and wary with the loss of him.

I stole the picture and others like it he had stacked in lazy piles around his house. I also pocketed the bracelet left behind in his bathroom that was next to a toothbrush with her name written on the handle. I imagined squatting over it on the toilet and peeing on the bristles like it was a pregnancy test. Even now, I'm not sure what stopped me. Maybe because I knew that it wasn't her fault. Sure, I could scramble to the top of some moral high ground and reason that she had gotten involved with a married man—*my* married man—and he welcomed it because he just needed someone to distract himself from loneliness and misery. But it was more complicated than that. Isn't it always more complicated than that?

For a week afterward, I couldn't eat. My chest swelled with a tennis ball-sized lump of grief that wouldn't let food pass through my esophagus. I heaved through tears, took long drives with the windows down to feel the wind in my hair, the loose strands nipping at my raw cheeks. I chain-smoked on my back porch and I blocked, unblocked, and re-blocked his number. Even then, I couldn't walk away. Even then, I went back to him, opened my heart, professed a love that I wasn't so sure I still knew.

We were supposed to be on a date of sorts, an effort to reconcile, start over, get to know each other again. In preparation, I had touched up my makeup and put on a cute top, ran a brush through my hair to calm the waves. He had put on a wrinkled oversized T-shirt and stained paints and answered the door in a haze. He had fallen asleep after work, he said, and it had morphed his overgrown hair into a boyish mess. On his coffee table was a Mary Kay bag with men's face wash, which meant she had been there recently, even though he had assured me they were taking a hiatus until he could decide if he could make it work with me.

I should have left then. Instead, I asked if I could fix his hair for him just as I had done so many times when we were together. I wetted a brush under the running faucet and tried to smooth down his cowlicks. When he suggested two possible places for dinner, I chose the one that I thought would be darker on the inside. I wanted to be seen with him, but I didn't want him to be seen with me.

"You're not coming in?" he asked after dinner when I pulled the car into the driveway and wished him a good night instead of turning off the ignition.

I tried to explain to him why I couldn't be with him anymore in the way he wanted me to be. If we were going to move toward a reconciliation, I told him, we need to work on having a relationship, not just having sex. "Besides," I said. "I know you're still seeing Tess. Who else would have given you Mary Kay products?"

He shook his head. "She broke it off."

"When?"

"Sunday."

It was Wednesday.

He looked sad, young, like he was being scolded. It was the look of man who felt defeated. It was the same look that always stirred compassion in me.

After loss there was resilience. There were nights on the couch crying in the blue light of the television, knocking over the lamp in my sleep, and awaking from a dream where I thought he was climbing in through the window, but it was just the lampshade teetering over the ledge of the end table, the stretched cord the only reason it hadn't tumbled to the floor.

It was a risk to love him again.

"Did you tell her you were fucking me, too?" I asked.

"You really messed her up when you called her my mistress," he said. "She can't even handle it when I mention your name."

His empathy lies with her, a self-proclaimed wounded soul who has lived a hard life. He worries about her well-being and comforts her the same way he comforts himself, with hedonism at the expense of everyone else, me in particular.

The truly wounded don't speak of their pain. It doesn't become grounds for spewing tantrums into the wind, for screaming into the noise. The truly wounded find refuge in their suffering because at least it gives them something to feel.

I conceded to go inside for a few minutes and cuddle with him because I knew he needed the comforting. We were two people who used to love each other but had been no good together. Sitting with him in the restaurant had been, for me, a complex mix of boredom, resentment that he had moved on, and wonder as to whether he felt anything for me anymore or if he ever had.

His body covered mine as we lay together on the couch. He pulled my shirt off, and I removed his so we could feel our bodies skin-to-skin, and I settled into the familiarity of him. He kissed my neck. I combed my fingers through his hair and lightly scratched my nails across his back.

Then, he bit me. On my shoulder, his kissing mouth parted and grazed my skin with his teeth. I arched my back, writhing under him as if to say, *Again, again.*

He bit me again, his beard—longer than I had ever seen it—tickling my collar bone.

My body shuddered. *Again*, it said.

He kissed my mouth, my neck, and continued to latch his teeth onto my skin. Nerves exploded into sirens and my brain shut down until everything existed only in that moment of his amatory gnawing.

Did Tess teach him to do that? Had he bitten *her*? Did he know how it would make me feel? Did he ever know how anything would make me feel?

I would have known he had slept with her even if he hadn't told me. Some things about his behavior had changed. His focus was elsewhere, his longevity needed coaxing. He hooked my ankles around his legs when he climbed on top of me. He was more attentive in some ways, yet he no longer orgasmed more intensely when I dug my manicured nails into his back. She was a welder. She didn't have nails. He no longer gripped the back of my hair and tugged when he came. Her hair was short. I gathered his face into my chest when I straddled him to bring him closer to my heart, but instead he remarked endlessly about the size and shape of my tits. Her breasts, like her body, were small. *You have such pretty eyes,* he said. So does she, I thought. So does she.

MARKED

"Wear your heart on your skin in this life."
—SYLVIA PLATH, *JOHNNY PANIC AND THE BIBLE OF DREAMS*

The springtime Mississippi air was making my hair frizz and my bangs curl, and I looked younger—felt younger—than anyone else in the dance club. I was nineteen, Lisa was twenty-four, and it was spring break for both of us on the cusp of Mardi Gras 2000. We were dressed in matching backless shirts and short skirts that we had bought together that afternoon in anticipation of our night out.

Lisa's outfit showed off her man-in-the-moon tattoo on her shoulder blade and the compliments from others led to revealing her zodiac tattoo—Leo surrounding Cancer—on her lower back that was slightly covered by the ambivalent fabric flitting her skin with each movement. I hung back and watched her soak in the attention from southern men, her hair straight and appearing redder than mine under the deceptive club lights, even though she was actually blonde.

I shifted in my basic pumps, my arches aching, and wished I had paid the money for knee-high boots like Lisa's. I felt the music pulse through me. I longed to dance, but there was no way I was going to venture out onto the floor by myself, and there was no way Lisa was going to dance without more drinks in her bloodstream or a man clinging to her hips.

She turned and looked at me over her shoulder before directing her voice to the friend of a man who had his mouth up against her ear. "She has a tattoo also." Then she turned her face back to the man in her neck, her eyes hidden behind closed lids.

I angled toward the friend, who was shorter than me and coated in heavy cologne, and flashed my shoulder in his direction, my arm draped across my chest so my polished fingernails could position themselves just above the black etchings of my tattoo.

He swirled the pad of his index finger over my skin, and I felt bile burn my throat. I glanced toward Lisa, but she was smiling into a muscular Bulgarian's mouth.

"Oh, it's a tiger face, huh?" The finger probed me again and settled on the nose. "Are you going to shade it in at all? I mean, it's still an outline, isn't it?"

To him, my tattoo was unfinished. I was unfinished.

—

My hand found its way under my sleeve and cupped the tender skin at the top of my arm, just under my shoulder, that was healing from the black outline of a tiger head tattoo, a Valentine's Day gift from Mark. I was starting to regret the design, something I chose hastily from a flash book ten minutes before my appointment. At first, I had wanted a butterfly. Ultimately, I had no idea what I wanted.

"Don't pass out," I said to Mark. I stretched my legs out flat in front of me, like I was seated in a dentist's chair, while a stranger shaved my arm with a dry disposable razor.

"I won't," the man said before Mark could respond, his eyes dancing between strands of long curly hair that hung over his face. They were the only words he spoke until the end of the appointment when he turned to Mark and asked for fifty dollars, paid in cash.

Finally, he covered my arm in plastic wrap and taped it down with masking tape before handing me a piece of paper with care instructions.

"That's it?" I expected more. I expected nothing.

I followed Mark out the front door and climbed into the passenger seat of his white Buick. It wasn't until I was buckling my seatbelt that I realized—for the first time in our relationship—he hadn't opened the door for me.

⁓

At the end of my spring break trip with Lisa, I traced the outline of comedy and tragedy masks from a plastic cup tossed from a parade float onto a piece of office-grade copy paper. When I returned to Michigan, I paid sixty dollars for a man with a soft mohawk and gray eyes so sexy and so intense he made me sweat, to ink the design into my back left shoulder, shading it heavily with bright colors that have since faded into an afterthought.

The tattoo shop I went to was on the outskirts of my college town in a building that looked like a weekend rental cabin from the outside. On the inside, however, it was clean and updated with flash boards on the wall to provide design options for the impulsive. The staff was less than friendly initially; the tattoo artist wouldn't even speak to me directly. Instead, he would consult on my design through his girlfriend, a former meth addict—"crank" she called it—who now made body jewelry and handled all his negotiations. I desperately sought their acceptance, to be welcomed by them for reasons I didn't know and couldn't explain.

For the year that followed, the muses Melpomene and Thalia from ancient Greek theater watched from my shoulder blade with the greatest range of human emotions as I caught what is known as "the fever." I spent so much time in that tattooist's chair that the ink stink mixed with my blood became a home place comfort.

I spent two hours in the chair for my arm band where he shaded the circles to look like bubbles without asking me first if I would mind. The rose tattoo on my foot—an homage to my trailer park upbringing—took a mere forty-five minutes. Long before lower-back tattoos were called "tramp stamps," I sat for mine for more than three hours, my pants low around my hips, and my ass crack in plain view of anyone who walked through the shop door. Every hour we took a ten-minute break, and I would angle toward the mirror to watch the design—a face that's a half-sun and half-moon surrounded by vines—fill space the size of a dessert plate on my skin. It didn't heal within a day like the others. Instead, it gelled and gooed and kept me awake for two long, hot July nights before it finally scabbed over. For a week afterward, the inside waistbands of all my pants were coated with colorful flakes as the shimmer of healing skin shined through and the scabs faded away.

Finally, a guy I had been sleeping with spent the weekend with an ex-girlfriend instead of me, and I retaliated by inking purple irises across my chest and piercing my nose, both in the same visit. The iris piece was done by someone new, someone who had never inked me before. It's a little sloppy, slightly crooked, and the only tattoo I can say I often regret. It represents haste, disillusionment, disappointment, and distrust, when it should represent independence and feminism and individualized power.

After that, ten years of tattoo silence.

~

"You gotta meet her," Mark said. He was talking about Kim, a woman he had met in a leather store where she worked while he was shopping for a jacket to accessorize his new motorcycle.

I was sitting on the edge of his bed while he stood in front of me waving his hands about as he tended to do when he told stories that weren't the complete truth, as though his grand gestures would distract me from his lies. For most of our relationship, it worked.

"I think you'll get along great. She's really cool."

I nodded. I had been really cool once, too.

"She has these tattoos on both her arms. Right here," he clutched a bicep, "And here," he clutched the other one.

I studied his bare skin and tried to imagine it female, tried to imagine it something other than freckled and pale. I nodded again.

"So, yeah. Really cool." He swiped his tongue across his lips until they blushed a deeper shade of pink.

Maybe he thought I would find Kim as cool as he did because I had longed for more designs of my own. It was second semester of my freshman year of college, and—aside from my roommates—I hadn't made any friends, hadn't connected with anyone on my 20,000-student campus because I spent the weekends with my boyfriend instead of going to parties. Mark was older, more experienced, a college drop-out who lived an hour away. He was an adult, and being with him made me feel like an adult, too.

⁓

There is a dichotomy between shame and pride. I had a secret. I still do. I walk into a classroom in pressed trousers and cardigan sweaters, and my appearance barely makes an impression on my students. That is until I watch their eyes shift from the handouts they take from me to the tattoo on my wrist. They move their surprised gaze to my face as though they have realized my humanity for the first time. I adjust my shirt to keep the irises from peeking out of the collar, but not for any reason other than I don't want the questions, the disbelief, or the distracted gawking.

I give workshops, presentations, trainings, all as a professional who appears professional. Underneath those layers, though, my skin sings a different song, a ballad of many verses comprised of love, pain, mistakes, imprinted memories.

I keep hidden, but I often wonder, are people more or less likely to listen to me if I give them something to look at?

When it comes to tattoos—particularly *my* tattoos—it seems everyone has an opinion, a comment, a critical remark. My mom preferred the piercings because those could be removed; she hoped I would outgrow them, and eventually I did. My dad preferred the tattoos. They could be covered up. They often were. If he didn't see them, then they didn't exist.

The summer after my freshman year of college, I bent over to pick up piles of gifts to carry them outside for my dad's backyard birthday party. Aunt Sue yanked the back of my shirt up while I was still getting a grip on the wrapped packages and tissue paper-filled gift bags and revealed the brightly colored piece on my lower back.

"Stop desecrating your body," she admonished, followed by, "it's pretty, though."

I waited until she stomped back through the kitchen before smoothing my shirt down and making my way outside.

In exam rooms where I'm cold, wearing a stiff paper gown, and often kept waiting, nurses have a habit of swooping in without apology, exposing my skin to poke it with a syringe or wrap a cuff around my arm, and reacting to the designs they reveal. During my first visit to a gynecologist's office, just before scooting down on the table, the nurse, hasty and impatient with my modesty, exclaimed, "How many *tattoos* do you *have*?" as the doctor pulled the gown away to check my breasts for lumps and exposed the irises stretched across my sternum.

After that, I found a different doctor whose nurse, if she notices my tattoos, says nothing.

Facedown on a massage table in a darkened room that is heavy with lavender oil, the masseuse will slip in the room after knocking lightly and fold back the top sheet. Often, she compliments the designs she sees, but in doing so, draws attention to the version of me that I am on the table to forget: the physical me, the "me" of the body.

The summer I spent a month teaching English in China, I wore crewneck T-shirts to cover as much as I could, but there was always an armband peeking out, and the rose on my foot was exposed by my sandals. Nobody said I had to stay covered, but I learned during our orientation conference call to err on the conservative; shorts should extend to mid-thigh or lower, flip-flops were out of the question. They didn't say anything about tattoos, and I didn't ask. I just assumed, as I always did, to cover up.

In China, the kids thought I was born that way. My tattoos were as foreign to them as my pink-tinted skin and my red hair which they always described as "yellow," or blonde because I'm white. We Americans. We all look alike.

—

"Look at that girl with a tiger on her arm." Mark would purse his lips with pride, even flap his eyelids a little as though he had eyelashes. I don't know if he ever liked the tattoo itself, but he seemed to revel in it, the visible mark he left on me. The pleasure in his face when he commented on my tiger tattoo was unmatched by any other look of adoration that he ever gave me.

In the beginning, I would smile back and run my fingertips over the tiger's face, noting how the swelling had gone down, how

MELISSA GRUNOW

the ink had become just as much a part of the skin as my freckles and a fine layer of baby-fine hair that grew back soft, even after the tattooist had shaved it off. As the spring moved into summer and Mark met Kim, I often answered his "look at that girl" comment with annoyed impatience. Didn't he have anything new to say?

The more Mark talked about Kim, the less I trusted his intentions, and I asked him accusatory questions about her and her role in his life. At first, he gave me reassuring answers, and I longed for the surge of love I felt when he set out to prove that, as he said one night, "No one can hold a candle to you." I actively sought the dramatic love depicted in romantic comedies because I was immature, just like our relationship.

Fourth of July weekend, I stared out the car window scanning the freeway for Mark's red motorcycle. He and Josh wore helmets with darkened visors to shield the sun as they headed to a northern Michigan lake somewhere unfamiliar to me. Rather than inviting me onto the back of his motorcycle, Mark pushed me to ride with Kim who drove Josh's car. I wanted to drive, to have some control over the situation, but I had never learned how to drive a manual transmission. Kim knew how, a skill that no doubt impressed Mark who saw me as more naïve with each passing day.

We stopped at a restaurant somewhere near Higgins Lake. The four of us sat in a row at the bar because the tables were full, and I hoped I wouldn't get carded just for sitting there. I was always the only person in the group who was still under twenty-one, and everyone liked to overlook the limitations that created. Everyone, that is, except me.

"This girl has the prettiest tattoo on her arm."

I turned toward the voice and saw an overweight man sitting on the stool next to Kim, pointing to the blue swirls on her skin and talking to no one in particular.

Kim sat with her elbows on the bar and took another bite of her turkey wrap. "You should see the one on my back," she said as she turned around and the pulled the hem of her shirt up past her bathing suit strap. The slight outline of her ribs was visible through her tanned skin. The tattoo was another swirl of colors, a simplified knock off of Van Gogh's *Starry Night*. I didn't know that then. Like her, I just thought it was pretty.

The man took advantage of Kim's self-exposure and studied the image carefully while she chatted with him about where we were from and our plans to spend the afternoon on a boat and watch the fireworks over the water as the sun went down.

"She has one, too." Kim nodded her head toward me, and I—reluctantly—pulled up the sleeve on my T-shirt. I wanted to go home.

He barely looked, barely nodded a courtesy nod. It wasn't at all like Kim's. I wasn't at all like Kim. She knew it, I knew it, and most importantly, Mark knew it.

Years after we broke up, Mark and I reconnected briefly on social media, then in a coffee house, then at an expensive restaurant with linen table cloths and bottle service.

I sought him out to finally hear his truth about Kim. I wanted to know if what I could see of her then was what he came to see later. Yes, he said. She was exactly the person you thought she was. Yes, he confirmed. I did date her after we broke up. Yes, he admitted. It may have happened before you left. It would have happened anyway.

There are still questions I will always wonder. "So how do you feel about her tattoos now? Still think they're cool? Still think she's cool?"

They are questions I will never ask because, as much as I wonder, I fear what I might learn from the answer.

Instead, I unfolded the cloth napkin into my lap and sipped an overpriced glass of wine on a Sunday afternoon, wondering how long it would be before Mark asked about the tiger tattoo on my arm that was no longer.

—

College came and went and then graduate school, and I was on the job market with nothing to wear to interviews. I had difficulty shopping and dressing for work and special occasions. It occurred to me early on that men put on more clothes when they're dressing up; women take them off and bare their legs, their arms, their shoulders, their backs. Bare skin is supposed to be sexy.

For me, skin equated to something else entirely. It revealed the decisions and secrets of my past, and a tattoo peeking out from a neckline or too-short shirt sleeve invited interrogations from people who wouldn't feel the same compulsion to ask such personal questions otherwise. My body remained unsettled and reshaped itself with countless rounds of weight gain and weight loss, the designs on my skin expanding and contracting like springs.

"Aren't you afraid of what they'll look like when you're older?" Really translates to, "Aren't you afraid of what you'll look like when you're old?"

Of course I am. Of course I do.

—

My ex-boyfriend Raul hated my tattoos, as did his mother. His stepfather Bill—who was also my boss—barely noticed if they showed through the fabric of my casual office clothing. There was no office rule about appearance, no specific dress code to speak of. Even so, Raul didn't even know that I had them until he saw me with my shirt off.

"They look so trashy," he would often say as we lay next to each other, partially clothed and vulnerable.

I could only shrug off his comments for so long. The longer we dated, the more controlling he became, and the more I longed to please him as I struggled with my own issues of self-confidence. I wanted someone in my life to be happy with the person I was. I longed for the proverbial "clean slate" that would take away the markings of my past and give me a second chance at something I couldn't yet define.

I was living in Ohio while Raul stayed in New Mexico, and the berating about my physical appearance grew worse with the distance. I would plan trips to visit him and would be met with a laundry list of improvements I had to make to myself as time went on.

One of the things on that list was tattoo removal. I had five tattoos by that point and the cost of laser removal was more than double my annual salary as a graduate assistant teaching three writing classes a year. An internet search for at-home tattoo removals compelled me to spend $99 on a serum applied with a brush—much like rubber cement—that was supposed to seep into the skin and bring the ink to the surface. Then all I had to do was wipe it clean.

I tried it on my tiger tattoo first and gritted through the burning sensation as my epidermis turned red, then bubbled, and finally, I had to blot it with a dampened paper towel as a reprieve from the pain. I lost count of how many applications I tried, but it didn't make a difference. The tattoo didn't bleed out. Instead, the skin blistered, scabbed, and healed, leaving a muddy scar on my skin.

Eventually, Raul and I broke up. Even though he had made me self-conscious about the tattoos that I had, it didn't stop me from getting three more in the years that followed. After two of my two cats died, I got paw prints and a purple flower on my left ankle to commemorate them. It was the first tattoo

I'd had in more than a decade, but the ink smell and buzzing of the gun were comforting in their familiarity. It was a new tattoo artist who had me lay on my side on a table while he gripped my foot and dug in. The vibration shivered up my leg each time he pressed into my ankle bone. It was a sensation I had never experienced, a pain that made me want to laugh and scream, an agonizing tickle. My reaction was embarrassing; I had always prided myself on being able to sit for a tattoo, no matter where it was or how long it took.

—

I wanted a cover-up for the tiger tattoo but lost my nerve the first time I wandered into a shop to inquire about it. Instead, I left forty-five minutes later with a nautical star tattooed inside my left wrist, the inspiration origin of it unknown to me.

With the tattoo bandaged, I came home to find my room-mate sitting at the dining room table. Joe didn't even greet me before he asked, "What happened to your arm?"

I didn't think he believed my response until I showed him that it was a tattoo and not a suicide attempt. Even then, the reassurance was partial.

"A nautical star?" Nick scoffed when I showed him later that night. "How original."

I shrugged. "I wanted a star."

He lay next to me with his shirt off, a giant tree expanding across his soft, pale chest, rooted in a woman with red hair who was draped in white around her hips and holding an apple. On his back stretched giant angel wings and "life" in Hebrew was inside his left wrist. I got tired of seeing those images. What at first appeared brave and daring and creative eventually came to be indicative of his desire for attention and affection. The idea of tattoos as sexy invites the gaze of others, side glances, blatant stares. There were even attempts at touching, to trace outlines with fingertips, to marvel at how the skin felt no different at sustaining such trauma.

He reveled in it. He sought the attention, the gaze from others. The questions and comments that made me want to cover up encouraged him to show off. His markings made others pay attention, and he thrived on their currency.

I didn't know that the new piece on my wrist was a nautical star or even what nautical meant. I had to look it up, scrolling through images and links to articles. At first, all explanations pointed to someone who had served in the Navy or was somehow affiliated with sea life. Lake-locked in Michigan probably didn't mean the same thing, and I felt a twinge of imposter shame. But then I found an article that specifically defined the placement of the star on the left wrist aligned with the thumb—as mine was—meant that the star was supposed to act as a positive guide for the future. I could live with that.

The final tattoo wasn't really a new piece, but instead, the cover-up of my tiger face tattoo that I had wanted for years. It's nearly a half sleeve now of three flowers, waves, and a train bell. It's better suited to who I am and what I want, but there is still the face of the tiger visible beneath the center of the sunflower, the stripes still unable to pass as a seed head. It will take more time in the chair attempting to communicate a version of myself that has not yet taken shape but will be someone who can grow from, rather than wallow in, regret.

TRAIN GONE

"The whole of life is about another chance, and while we are alive, till the very end, there is always another chance."
—JEANETTE WINTERSON, *WHY BE HAPPY WHEN YOU COULD BE NORMAL?*

1.

We stand in drizzling rain outside a Chinese cafe, slightly shivering in thin jackets. The parking lot is framed by shops that have closed down for the night. Aside from the staff inside the restaurant rolling silverware into napkins and mopping the floor, it seems we are the only people who haven't rushed home. He's finishing a story that started while we were still sitting at the table and there is—for the first time all night—momentary silence.

"So," he says, the tone of his voice shifting to a slower gear. "This was fun."

I nod and smile a little to encourage him to go on. "It was."

"We should do it again."

"Sure," I say. "Any time."

"But I have to tell you—" he begins.

I stiffen a little. There is always a moment during a first date when each person decides if the time spent sharing a meal is going to lead to meaningful time together in the future. Our moment is now, in the parking lot, in the rain, before we have declared if our meal was actually a date. While I'm still unsure about him and us, he seems to have already reached a conclusion about what could happen next.

"I haven't dated since probably graduate school," he continues.

I steady my face and wait for more. There is always more to the story.

"So," he pauses. "I guess I don't know what that means."

He's forty-nine years old. I do the math quickly and realize he hasn't dated since the nineties, the decade of my childhood. "It doesn't have to mean anything," I say. I pause for a moment and ask the question I probably shouldn't ask. "Why so long?"

"There was a relationship," he starts. "I'd rather not get into the details now, but let's just say things didn't end well. So I decided not to date for a while, and that turned into years."

I nod a little, trying to imagine the details that he won't disclose. I rock my body to quiet the dozens of thoughts bouncing around inside my mind, including one tiny alarm bell.

"There's an expression in ASL," he says as he makes the sign. "It literally translates to, 'Train gone.' Typically it's used when someone comes in late to the conversation, and the person telling the story doesn't want to repeat everything. It's like when we say, 'You missed the boat.' So, I guess you could say, in this case, I missed the boat." He smiles as if it's enough of a reason.

"Train gone," I repeat, kicking at the asphalt.

2.

My neighbor catches my attention one morning before I leave for work. "I wanted to let you know that someone tried to break into our house Sunday night," he says.

I set my coffee mug on top of the car and walk toward him across my front yard. "What happened?"

"My wife had fallen asleep in front of the TV. Around one o'clock in the morning she woke up to someone fiddling with the front door. They were twisting the knob," he reaches his hand out to demonstrate, "but the door was locked. Then she heard them walk around the side, through the gate, and try the side door."

I stand there staring at him. I look to his house and imagine a shadowy figure lurking between our two homes, testing his locks just below my bedroom window.

"We called the police," he says. "But by the time they got here, whoever was trying to get in was long gone."

For weeks, every creak, every squeak, and I'm looking over my shoulder or around a corner, or not, for fear of what I might find. The *thump* of my cats jumping from the furniture to the floor sounds like footsteps—a person—moving about on the other side of the wall.

I come home from work to find my laptop open. I find the basement door unlatched. I wake up to find I've left the door unlocked all night. Do I invite these opportunities to feel afraid, to create a threat in my own home?

I keep mace in my bedside table, mace that was given to me by my parents one Christmas to carry when I went running at night. Now the canister rests in the drawer, the red button just inches from my head each night as I wake to wind whipping against the vinyl siding, raindrops on the shingles, the window panes shuddering from the reverberations of a passing train. When I do sleep, I keep the light on.

3.

Venice is the first stop in Italy. We will have a guided tour that includes St. Mark's Square, a gondola ride, and a glass blowing demonstration followed by a lunch of paella and wine, and then we're on our own to wander the city until after dark. In the morning, we will go to Verona and then on to Florence, Pisa, Assisi, Rome, and, finally, The Vatican.

Someone asks about a map and Antonio, our tour guide, waves his hand dismissively and croons, "Get lost in Venice," before handing out the maps anyway. I tuck mine away in my messenger bag, certain I will need it. Getting lost seems like bad advice.

Dave shifts in the bus seat next to me and makes a joke about how to file a missing person's report in Italian. A few of the other tourists laugh, but Antonio doesn't. He looks at Dave and then at me and kind of smiles as if to ask how in the world we ended up together. The others on the trip know Dave as my live-in boyfriend, but our relationship had effectively ended weeks prior. It was too late to cancel his ticket or transfer it to someone else, however, so here he was on what could have been a romantic tour of Italy, but instead, we were just trying to tolerate each other.

I just want this trip to Italy to be over and done with, I had written in an email to my friend.

She had offered to go on the trip with me, to even pay some kind of ticket change fee, if possible. *It would be a lot less stress on you during the trip, but would put you in a position to take on the stress of addressing him now instead of later.*

I actually just called the tour company and they can't make any changes this late. Otherwise, I would totally be up for that, I responded the next day. *We got into it last night and I basically told him that he's living in a fantasy, that his whole world revolves around him and I am tired of being a supporting actress in the movie that's constantly playing in his head. Later, he asked me why I was trying to sabotage our relationship. Then he actually started asking about past relationships to see if there was some kind*

MELISSA GRUNOW

*of "pattern" that he could identify, as if this is the way I typically
operate, as if he has done nothing wrong.*

Dave says something about not having enough room for
his legs or his knees. I ignore his complaints with a rhetori-
cal shrug and stare out the window. He is broke, and though
the trip is mostly inclusive, it won't cover everything he will
want to do or see or eat or drink. I have very little disposable
income of my own, and I know I will be returning from Italy
in emotional and financial debt.

4.

The subway is the heart of New York City. Even when we walk
in tandem along the sidewalk, I can feel it pulse beneath our
feet, flowing fast toward its next destination. There are posters
everywhere with the tagline, "If you see something, say something." They compel New Yorkers to assist people in distress,
to report suspicious activity and emergencies to the conduc-
tor. Most people, however, pay no attention to those around
them. It's a place of escape and anonymity.

Passengers gather on plastic seats or cling to chrome poles
and brace themselves against the inertia pull and tug with each
stop along the way. Joe stands near the door, even though
there are seats available and the ride into Chinatown is a long
one. I opt to sit and realize almost immediately why the car
is only half full and most people are standing. The stench of
the homeless man across the aisle reaches me immediately. I
turn my head to the side, but it doesn't help. He is hunched
over with his head between his legs and wearing a dirty jacket
inside out. His body sways a little with the movement of the
train as he dangles like a puppet on slack strings. The floor
around him is littered with discarded fried chicken nibbled
down to the bone.

We exit the train at the last stop, and I hesitate for just a second to see if the man will sit up, gather his things, and make his way off the train, but he doesn't.

I say nothing to Joe, to anyone, until later that night when we are sipping craft beer at a hipster bar around the corner from his apartment.

"I worry I should have said something," I say. "What if he wasn't okay? What if he needed help?"

"The first time you see something like that, it worries you," Joe says. "But then you get used to it. He might be okay. He might not be. But whether you told someone or not, you will never know."

5.

At the Tiki Bikini Hut in Nassau, a Bahamian man makes a comment about the Mercedes on my finger and says, "I would have married him, too, had he given me a rock like that."

I turn to my husband and smile because that is how I should respond to such a statement. I take another sip of the piña colada out of the coconut I have to hold with both hands, the one chopped open and carved into a drinking vessel with a machete by a man behind the counter. Flies and wasps swarm us, seeking the sweetness of the fruit and alcohol that trickles down the blenders and sullies the counters. Beyond the hut is a public beach littered with white bodies, and beyond that, a blue-green ocean.

Two months married and we are finally on our honeymoon, instead of back in Michigan and Illinois celebrating Christmas with our families. We are away from the pressures of being newlyweds, from the well-meaning people who start every conversation with, "So, how's married life?" I am tired of answering that question. The trip has been a reprieve because everyone around us, it seems, is on their honeymoon, too. Newly married is common here, yet still recognized as something to celebrate.

It's the first and only day of five that we leave the confines of our all-inclusive resort. We didn't have enough cash to pay for a taxi into town, and I was nervous we wouldn't be able to pay for the shuttle that would take us back to the airport. It was the same concern that gave me reservations about going downtown at midnight for Junkanoo, a parade and street festival in The Bahamas to celebrate Boxing Day. We woke up early that morning, and every morning, to catch the breakfast buffet and vacate our room so the cleaning staff could change out the towels that remained perpetually damp in the Caribbean humidity. I had spent most of the day lying on the beach or next to the pool, flipping through the pages of a book I had already finished as Chris wandered off, sometimes for hours, returning without an explanation for where he had been. By the time he had suggested going downtown for the festival, I was tired. We couldn't get dinner reservations at any of the resort restaurants, so he stomped off to take a nap, and I ate carved turkey from the Christmas buffet, alone. I didn't want to leave, to be out all night without money and without any certainty that the bus would be running to bring us back. For all his assurances that it would be fine, that we should just go, I couldn't trust that he had a plan, that he had considered the reasons that were giving me pause. So, instead, we fought. The heat, the sun, the free alcohol, the heavily chlorinated pool, the crowded resort, had all gotten to the both of us, and we fought. We yelled. He pinned me to the bed to calm me down, he said, as I gasped, struggled free, called him a sonofabitch, and swung my arm until my hand collided with the side of his head.

I'll never forget his expression, his face red, the lines around his mouth and eyes etched deeply, his teeth framing a sob that couldn't escape.

It wasn't until he smashed and shattered the glass top on the dresser that he fled the room, his camera bag slung over his shoulder. Moments later, there was a gentle knock at the door, and I came face-to-face with resort security and a Nassau police officer. Someone had called in a noise complaint, he said. Is everything okay?

I sat on the edge of the bed while he filled out the incident report and someone from maintenance cleaned up the broken glass shards from the tile floor, taking great care to find every piece so we wouldn't cut our feet. We would have to pay for the damage when we checked out, they said.

Where is husband now? the officer asked.

I shook my head and shrugged. I don't know, I said, which was the truth. Maybe he had gone to Junkanoo alone. Maybe he was in one of the resort bars. Maybe he was walking in the dark along the beach. It was all possible.

We're supposed to be on our honeymoon, I whispered.

He patted my shoulder and his voice was soft with reassurances. He didn't offer congratulations or ask about married life like everyone else. He offered a kind of understanding that I couldn't yet reconcile.

Nobody warned us marriage could be like that.

At the Tiki Bikini Hut, we spend our remaining forty dollars on the coconut drinks, not realizing when we ordered them how much they cost or that this open air bar on the beach was cash only. I gaze at my ring and then up at him before leaning forward to kiss him on the temple, letting my lips linger, the affection an act of love I would just have to endure.

6.

He says, "I'm sorry," but he doesn't mean it to be an apology. He means, "I'm frustrated and feel as though I've failed you. I've failed myself. I've failed again."

It's a child's sorry, an apology to ward off anticipated punishment. Except he's not my child.

I clean, organize, and maintain the house, and he walks through a room dropping things along the way, kicking off his shoes, settling into a place he has now called home, a place that I have enjoyed most when I've been here alone.

I feel frustrated with him, when his messy corner of the bedroom grows larger piles, and I can't see the work I put in just weeks ago when we sat in that corner together, in that room together, and I helped him sort through the mess, thing by thing, so he doesn't hit himself in the head, so he doesn't apologize and tell me, "I'm not worthy of you."

I don't like to clean. And when I have to, I raise my voice and lower my tone to a snappy growl, just like my mother. *Just like my mother.* Just like my mother with a broom or a mop or a dusting rag in her hand or her arms so full of discarded toys and shoes and strewn about coats that she can't open them for a hug. Not one second to pause and hug.

"Don't yell at me," he says. "You make my brain rattle." He shuffles in with his arms outstretched and his head down. He's sorry. I'm sorry.

But neither of us can change.

Tomorrow is my thirty-sixth birthday, the final year of my mid-thirties. This is my awkward age of adulthood where I am both entirely sure and terrified that I have become who I actually am. I have entered an age of personal quiet. Maybe I've always been here. Maybe I can never leave.

I can't go home. Not yet. My house is in transition. My husband of just ten months is moving out, or supposed to be, anyway, and I've escaped for the weekend to a campsite three hours away in search of solitude and a desperate attempt at quiet to sort my thoughts and make sense of my uncertain future.

Chopped birch wood burns in the fire pit, and the flame smells sweet and heavy, like buttercream frosting. I realize quickly that two bundles of birch and some glossy fliers as kindling aren't enough to get me through two nights. The logs burn down quickly and are nothing but a smoldering glow of ash just before dusk.

I take to the hiking trails to collect as much fallen dried wood as I can carry. It piles up quickly next to the pit, but once I get the fire going again, it seems to burn even faster than the birch. Two of the branches are still adorned with dried leaves, and they send the flames high. It's not completely dark yet, but too late to wander out again in search for more wood. I take the poker stick and break it down into three pieces then stack it carefully on top of the quiet flames. By the time it's fully dark, I will have only my lantern for light and only my sweatshirt for warmth.

In my tent that night, I dream I am being followed while I walk along an unknown street. When I ignore the pursuer and give my attention to other things—my cell phone, directions, stray receipts in my coat pocket—he falls into the shadows. When I finally turn to face him, he quickens his pace from the other side of the street, his loafers slapping against the concrete.

I force myself to scream, pushing an alarm from the back of my throat, and just before he grabs me, I wake up. The morning sky is periwinkle. Acorns fall from the trees and go *thunk* on the ground. It's like rain, but not rain. Ash from the fire coats the outside of my car in snow-like flakes that will never melt.

MELISSA GRUNOW

7.

We ride the subway everywhere in New York City. I keep my metro pass in an outside pocket of my purse and have it in hand, ready to slide through the turnstile before we approach. It needs to be done in one swift and confident motion or else risk creating a ricochet of stalled stops and screeching of sneakers against the stained concrete behind me. He is a real New Yorker now, and I resemble one by being aloof, lost in thought, and looking away before I make eye contact with strangers.

Joe jokes about how long it would take for me to lose my "Midwestern nice" if I made New York my home.

"You haven't lost yours," I tell him. "You're just more selective about who you share it with."

What I mean is, he's nice to me. He's kind and considerate but not affectionate. Not that he should be. He isn't my boyfriend or my lover. Though, the definition of us doesn't stop me from linking my arm with his when I get drunk, making the excuse that I need him to help me stay upright, to guide me along the sidewalk. I don't want to lose him, I reason, when he starts to walk too fast as he tends to do. One night I take his hand in mine, and he doesn't pull away. He tolerates me, endures my affection because he knows I adore him.

I also wonder if I actually know him. He doesn't brood anymore. He isn't sad. He isn't cocky to cover his personal uncertainties like he used to be. He is no longer young. He's increasingly well-traveled and knows more about so much that I am almost intimidated. When we venture out into the city, he leads me. I don't lead him.

He used to be open about his disagreements with me and my choices; his disappointment would linger on his face even if he didn't speak about it. It doesn't anymore. My vices are his.

At night I struggle to fall asleep. I blame the creaking futon each time I roll over or reposition myself. I blame the dry air from the radiator that fights the cold November night and the city noise cascading in through the open window. I blame the strangeness of a new place, that I drank too much, that I am excited for tomorrow. But really, it's because he is asleep in the next room, just on the other side of a closed door and everything smells like him in his apartment, and I miss him.

Anything I ask for, he complies. Wherever I want to go, he goes, too. He says yes. Always yes. Yes to everything, except when I ask to share his bed because I'm so desperate for the comfort that comes from the proximity of another person.

"I would rather you didn't," he says without a hesitation or a stumble.

In the morning, I pretend I said nothing. I had forgotten other parts of our conversations that had happened the night before, and so I pretend to forget *that*. I don't mention it, and neither does he. New York has humanized him without making him edgy. He doesn't have the hardness I would come to expect.

You know when police will comb a lake looking for bodies when someone has drowned? Before New York, I felt like the rake pulling through muck, moving slowly and coming up with nothing.

8.

On a water taxi in Italy heading away from Venice, I climb the steps to the upper deck to say goodbye to the city I've come to love in just two days. It's a windy, sunny day, and I can see the Venetian skyline in the distance getting smaller, nothing but sprawling water and wake between us.

I sit on a bench next our tour guide, Antonio. He turns to me and says, "Melissa, they built all of this for you," he gestures to the ancient architecture in the distance. "And once you leave, oomph!" He brings his hands from above his head to his lap to mimic their collapse.

Antonio is a charming Italian man who says charming things in an Italian accent, but more importantly, he doesn't ask about Dave, who I've left alone below the deck. Antonio is genuine, yet the idea of anything falling to destruction in my absence makes me laugh. I'm disillusioned from living a life that isn't real and hoping for relationships that don't come to fruition. Antonio isn't sexy, but I am still flattered, so I stay with him on the bench until the air becomes too cold and Venice disappears. When I stand to go back down to the lower deck, I don't say goodbye because I'm not ready to do so. Venice, from what I hear, is still standing.

9.

It's raining for the third day in a row, and I walk briskly toward my car with my head down. I open the passenger side door and toss in my bags, then walk around the back of the car, keys in hand. There's a van parked next to me, backwards, our driver's doors lined up side-by-side.

A tall, thin man wearing a black sweatshirt with the hood pulled over his head approaches his door at the same time I approach mine. "Oh, excuse me," I say as I turn my back to him, and reach for the handle to climb into my car first.

My head jerks backward, and my keys fall to the ground. The man has me by the back of the hair, his hand tangled in tight.

I twist. He starts to pull, to drag me, and I make myself as heavy as I can while trying to reach behind me to hit, scratch, claw. My fingertips brush against the cool metal of his zipper and drag along the fabric of his sweatshirt. My feet scuttle backward as he pulls me harder, and I can't stand up, I can't fall down.

Don't let them take you. Whatever you do, don't let them take you. The words pop into my head from a news broadcast or a self-defense lecture, I don't know for sure. I listen to the advice and remember the warnings, the statistics of women who are abducted and never return. *Fight like hell*, the voice says. *But don't let them take you.* My shoe grazes over my keys, and I kick them hard between my tires so that my car is not an option for him.

It's my last moment of clarity. The pain resonates through my skull to my neck and down my spine. I scream. I feel as though I am minutes, seconds, away from blacking out. I struggle, I grunt, I scream some more.

Through my tears and the rain, against the backdrop of the night sky, I see a clenched fist come toward my face. My eye explodes and explodes again, the fist pulling back and coming toward me over and over.

He doesn't speak. He continues to hit me to shut me up.

Bile collects in my throat and burns. I choke, cough, scream some more. My eyes close, and among the darkness are spots of brightness, like white twinkle lights against a dark house at Christmas. I raise my hands to my head and scratch at his clenched fist that's tangled in my hair, the other draped around my neck and squeezing, but I can't get in there, I can't unwrap the strands from around his fingers. I'm quiet as I struggle to breathe, the heels of my shoes dragging against the asphalt.

The pulling stops. I'm shifted sideways, then dropped to the ground, landing hard on the asphalt, tiny rocks scraping the palm of my hand, and I hear the soles of his shoes splash in

MELISSA GRUNOW

puddles as he runs off, spooked by shouting voices approaching from a distance.

The rain continues to fall, water from the parking lot seeps into my clothes, soaking me. I stand up, slowly, my knees untrustworthy. I sway and collapse against the bumper of my car. *The bumper.* I was dragged almost ten feet. In how much time? I can't be sure.

For months after, I need an escort every time I walk through a parking lot. I don't grocery shop at night. I don't leave my house after dark. I continue to sleep with the light on next to my bed.

10.

The lights inside the Chinese café go dark just before the few remaining staff exit out the front door. They turn and see us standing in the parking lot, though they don't look surprised that we are still wrapping up our end-of-date small talk. Neither one of us seems to know how to leave with an uncertain farewell. He's talking about the deaf summer camp he worked at in the Adirondacks in college, a long-winded answer to my inquiry about how he knows sign language. I nod along, listening without retaining the details because I'm already wondering if this will be one of those love stories of unlikely connection.

The wind blows my hair over my face, and I catch a whiff of my shampoo. Are men drawn to this scent? Or do I remind them of their mother or sister instead?

I shiver and zip my coat as high as it will go, and he suggests for the third and final time that we go our separate ways. We don't make definitive plans, but we do see each other again and again until there is one night when the date goes just a little too long, and we run out of things to talk about. I want to live moment to moment without jumping to what the future could look like for me and this other person, but I don't know how to stay focused on today. I want to confront obstacles in the relationship before there is even a relationship, and that frightens men. At least I believe it frightened him. I want to work toward something meaningful, toward something of validity. He is stuck on hugs of greetings and salutations, but nothing more. I'm too old to train someone how to be in a relationship, and he's far too old to learn. Our paths didn't cross at the right moment in our lives; with a seventeen-year age gap, it's unlikely they ever will.

In the car, though, I don't know any of this. Instead, I am filled with hope and wonder. He follows me for a few miles as we head back to the freeway, and I can see his headlights in my rearview mirror while we wait at a railroad crossing for a train to pass. He sends me a text message that we could have talked in the rain for another ten minutes, and I respond with something witty, possibly flirtatious, smiling to myself at our shared humor.

I turn down the radio so I can hear the whistle outside my closed window, three short and one long, and the chugging of a locomotive along the tracks, a bell ringing as it passes through town.

And then, train gone.

MELISSA GRUNOW

DISSONANCE

"Dieting is the most potent political sedative in women's history; a quietly mad population is a tractable one."
—NAOMI WOLF, *THE BEAUTY MYTH*

I wake up in the middle of the night and vomit. Sometimes my husband hears me and he knocks on the door, asks if I'm okay. By the time I come out of the bathroom, he is already back in bed sleeping so soundly that he doesn't stir when I settle in under the covers. Or he stirs just enough to drape his arm over my body, the weight of it heavy on my ribcage. I push him away and meet his grumbling with, "Don't push down on my stomach."

His fingers seek out the warmth between my legs, an unwelcomed touch.

"Cut it out," I insist and pull away again.

"Come *on*," he says. "We're married. This is what married people do."

If you hold your hand over a lit flashlight, you can see the blood in your palm.

When you drill through a knot on a plank of pine, the wood will bleed clear sap onto your fingers.

Only one of these facts is true. The other is a matter of perception.

Kinetosis—commonly known as motion sickness—is felt in the gut, but it actually happens in the labyrinth of the inner ear. The central nervous system is confused by conflicting messages from the senses that keep us balanced, thinking that we are moving when we are not. It doesn't know how to respond, so it sends a distress signal to various parts of the body, causing headaches, sweating, fatigue, dizziness, nausea, and vomiting.

As a child, I got car sick (or at least felt nauseous) on every road trip. My parents would stop for donuts on the way out of town, disappear inside, and return with a box of a mixed dozen: glazed, Boston cream, chocolate frosted, jelly-filled, crullers, and something with sprinkles. Donuts were only for travelling, so they were a treat, but they always made me feel sick. After a while, I stopped eating them while the rest of the family munched away, and I longed to stick my head out the window to escape the scent of fried dough and sugar that filled the car. The smell alone made me gag.

Sometimes the motion-induced nausea could be controlled as long as I looked out the window instead of down at a book. If I was lucky, I would sleep away the miles, my body swaying along with the gentle rhythm of the moving car.

There was a year when I ate nothing and ran long distances, when my body whittled down to the smallest size I have ever been. I think how easy it was to get dressed every morning, when everything in my closet looked good on me, when I looked good on me, when I could cross my legs without my top leg slipping off my bottom knee, when my left hip and my right knee didn't throb, ache, and tighten after being seated for a long time. Instead, if I stood up too quickly, the room would tilt and spin, the edges of my vision receding into darkness like burnt paper. The pit of my gut felt like a deepening cavity. I quieted the rumble by gulping large glasses of water, propped against the kitchen counter to prevent myself from tipping out of consciousness.

I cooked elaborate meals for dinner, plated them, and then dumped the whole thing into the trashcan, watched an hour or two of my day slide off the glass and listened for the inevitable *plop* as it landed in the bin and became garbage.

～

Food was always in abundance in my childhood home, even when everything else was minimal. We had a lot of people and not a lot of money, so basic necessities were scarce and cheap but the choices at mealtime were plentiful. Dinnertime was the only opportunity for greed as we were encouraged to help ourselves to seconds, to finish off the bowl or pan to avoid leftovers that would either be microwaved to mush a week later or forgotten about and discarded.

Cooking is a relaxing activity for my mom—at least, it is now. Feeding a family of seven in a modest kitchen was probably a daily stress, but it was normal. We ate together every evening and often had large breakfasts on Saturday mornings consisting of eggs, pancakes or waffles, sausage and bacon, and orange juice, a luxury over the glass of milk we drank with every other meal.

After I moved out, I started receiving cookbooks for Christmas nearly every year. They accumulated quickly, their spines lined up in a cabinet I cannot reach without a stool, the pages dusty and flat from endless non-use. When I cook, it's in large quantities and entirely utilitarian. Food in my refrigerator is stored in airtight containers that I eat for an entire week. Each weekend, I repeat the process of chopping, dicing, sautéing, mixing, and storing so that the containers are ready for me to zip into a cooler bag come Monday morning and eat at my desk during the workday.

Although dinnertime was an opportunity to indulge and gorge on food without shame or scolding, we otherwise had strict rules around food in my childhood home. There was food we were allowed to eat and food that was completely off-limits. The rules were not directly stated anywhere or written down; we just understood. Animal crackers and apples were a staple for afternoon snacks. If a box of granola bars or a bag of goldfish crackers showed up in the cupboard, we knew better than to even ask. As a teenager, I hoarded chocolate bars and butterscotch candy and hid them throughout my bedroom. I often stopped at a convenience store while walking to school and bought Pop-Tarts with the money I made babysitting, and later from my afterschool job.

We were allowed to drink Kool-Aid in the summer but never the cans of soda stockpiled in the basement that my mom bought in large quantities when it was on sale. Ice cream was an occasional after-dinner treat when I spooned a bowl for myself to eat while doing homework and a bowl for my dad to enjoy in front of the television. Fla-Vor-Ice pops were permitted, but we had to ask. They were rationed, the privilege revoked if we littered the yard or basement with the plastic casings.

Any access to treats was simply a temptation that would lead to trouble. Access to an abundance of food was a provision at mealtime but grounds for punishment if we consumed more than the unknown limit allowed.

For instance, I didn't remember eating all the cookies.

In the morning—after my parents finally allowed Rachel to sleep over, after I convinced them that the basement was clean enough, warm enough, inviting enough for us to huddle under sleeping bags on the floor—my mom screamed down the basement steps, "You ate *all* the chocolate chip cookies!"

My eyes opened first, and then Rachel's, and our eyes looked at each other's eyes, brown and sad and too cold, too scared, to come out of our sleeping bags and stare down the supposed empty container that sat atop the refrigerator.

I knew better than to respond to my mom's yelling; I also knew better than to ignore her. I was ashamed in front of my friend who had joined me in the kitchen after everyone went to bed and leaned against the counter next to me, pulling apart the thin, soft cookies, and chewing through the chewiness of them between sips of milk.

We had two each. Two. Maybe three. But most definitely no more than four.

"We didn't have that many," Rachel whispered to me, her face squished in defense.

I nodded. "I know."

Eight. We probably had eight cookies between us. Did we each grab one more before we headed back to the basement? Then okay, ten. Ten cookies. While we definitely hadn't eaten all of them, we had eaten too many. No one told us our limit, but we exceeded it anyway.

I wasn't allowed to have friends sleep over for a long time after that. The next time my parents baked cookies together, I wasn't allowed to have even one. That was the way it worked. There was no joy without consequence.

The stages of digestion are masticate, swallow, peristalsis, digest, absorb, and eliminate. This process is interrupted between the peristalsis and digestion stages, however, when fingers are shoved to the back of the throat and the meal is expelled up through the esophagus where the bile burns along the way and is forced out through the mouth and into a toilet. For me, this habit formed in college when I started swallowing diet pills (that have since been recalled because of their link to heart attacks), multivitamins, and even antibiotics. Sometimes the nausea was self-induced by mindlessly consuming excessive amounts of potatoes that I boiled, mashed, diced and baked, or fried. The starchy texture coated in butter and seasoned with garlic salt was cheap to purchase, a comfort to eat, and easy to prepare.

I kept the toilet clean for when I inevitably threw up into it. I still do.

Cognitive dissonance is the sense of anxiety that comes into play when we hold beliefs that are in conflict with our behavior. We know in our rational mind that what we are doing is somehow wrong, but we negotiate with ourselves to justify it. This happens through reductive rationalization, denial, and minimization of the hurt to self or others that the behavior could cause.

It occurs when edible food is tossed into the trashcan because we know that it's bad to waste food. It occurs when we binge because we know that eating should be purposeful and in moderation, rather than indulgent. It occurs when we are lazy in changing personal habits that we know will improve our quality of life in the end. It occurs when we shop in excess, sleep in excess, drink and smoke in excess, watch television in excess, experience physical pleasure in excess, and, of course, eat in excess.

Meat, especially red meat, has never agreed with me. I can feel it congeal inside of my body, my stomach distending to the point of discomfort whenever I eat it. I don't like how it looks when it's raw, how it smells while it's cooking, or that the smell would linger in my clothing long after the dishes were washed and the kitchen cleaned.

Becoming vegan, for me, was inevitable. Not just for health reasons (though it did lower my cholesterol from 210 to 140 in just a month), and not just for the betterment of the environment (though the meat industry is one of the greatest contributors to pollution and erosion on our planet), but because it's a diet built on restriction. It's not just cutting out meat; it's a complete elimination of all animal products and by-products, including those buried deep in the ingredients of pre-packaged and processed food. It curbs my impulse to gorge on salty fast food, to order any dish off of any menu in any restaurant, and keeps at bay the guilt I experience whenever I eat something that tastes like pleasure.

My husband was the embodiment of indulgence. He did what he wanted, when he wanted to do it, without guilt or thought of the impact it would have on those around him. I went into the marriage with a set of unstated and unwritten expectations for the two of us: to be married meant living as people who didn't hinge their decisions on desire. To do so was infantile, and we were adults.

I gained some weight after we moved in together, but he gained nearly fifty pounds. While I walked the dog to walk off the weight or pushed the lawn mower up and down the yard and imagined progress with each drip of sweat that soaked through my clothes, he stayed in bed for days, clicking through photos on his computer, preparing for something greater than he was capable. His ambition to become a photographer far surpassed his talents, but that didn't stop him from funneling all of his money into his art. It didn't stop him from financial and emotional dependence on me. Rather, it was his inherent expectation that I support him unconditionally, even if it meant sacrificing myself.

When we ate meals together, I prepared them. Sometimes an hour would pass between the time I told him dinner was ready and when he finally descended the stairs. Even then, he would eat slowly and in silence as though he were a child and I his mother, forcing him to clean his plate before he could go outside and play. When the meal was over, he would return to the bedroom and his computer while I was left to clean the kitchen and make meal preparations for the next day. When I finally grew tired of cooking for him, he would fill a grocery cart with bulk boxes of frozen food (mozzarella sticks, jalapeño poppers, pizza bagels, fish sticks), beer, energy drinks, ranch dressing, corn chips and queso, and toss everything into any space he could find in the kitchen when he got home. He didn't prepare meals so much as heat food in the toaster oven, all the while complaining that it took too long and why we didn't have a microwave?

Dirty dishes and empty beer bottles would pile up on the floor and table next to his side of the bed until I begged him to clean it up or finally cleaned it myself. He never stopped eating in the bedroom, though, not even when food or drinks spilled onto the carpet, not even when plates became so caked with old food that they had to be thrown away.

Sometimes I would eat his food in bed with him and we would watch television. I hated it, but I tolerated it because at least we were doing something together. "Can't we go for a hike? What about a bike ride?" I asked in the beginning and then eventually stopped asking. Either he was too tired from working, or he was laid off and trying to build his photography business. Regardless, there was always a reason to decline.

He got food poisoning once and blamed it on bad pizza, but he also hadn't washed his hands beyond rinsing off his fingertips after cleaning up dog waste in the yard. The air in our bedroom was thick and heavy under the weight of his fever sweats, shit, and vomit. I covered his forehead with a wet washcloth and rubbed his shoulders while he cried.

His sickness sickened me. He was the root cause of our collective illness, of parasites that lived in our intestines and devoured their hosts from the inside out. There was always something to blame for his suffering, the finger most often pointed at me. I swallowed my culpability and then vomited into the toilet while he slept. This went on during the last four months of our marriage as we became two people residing under the same roof who resented each other. We both stopped giving in the way that the other person wanted, withholding everything that brought the other person comfort, anything that made the other person feel loved.

"This is what married people *do*."

No. No it isn't.

The thing is, when you find out your husband has slept with someone else, the truth of your life together burrows itself down into the darkest part of you, bringing bile and anger to your throat until you choke on it. Your memories of his body writhing with yours become thoughts of him with her and you wonder if he is tender or animalistic. You wonder if she smells better, looks better, feels better than you.

It won't matter that your marriage began to end the day after your wedding when you fought over how his ex-girlfriend and bridesmaid denounced your relationship once again and you refused to stay silent about it any longer, that eight months later the two of you stopped having sex, that three months after that he moved out, then in another three months he filed for divorce and you were served papers in the rain so that the summons is forever crinkled from getting wet, that three months after that your divorce was finalized in front of a judge who intimidated him but not you, so you answered all of the questions during the ten-minute hearing until she dismissed you by saying, "Best of luck to you both."

None of that will matter because you were still married when he met this woman, still married when he kissed her on

New Year's Eve, and still married when he drove to Florida with her where they slept together for the first time.

You wonder if they were happy every moment of that trip or did he wander off and leave her alone on the beach for hours as he had done to you when the two of you were on your honeymoon in The Bahamas? Did he ignore her in favor of his cell phone or computer? Did he refuse to share meals with her where actual conversation and true human connection took place?

I don't force myself to throw up anymore because I don't need to do so. My body makes the decision to eliminate consumption for me. A lifetime of abuse has weakened my gastrointestinal system, and all stressful situations in my life attack my stomach first. There is nothing I can eat that doesn't require careful consideration in advance of the impact it may have on me later that day, the next morning, the rest of the week. Even eating vegan has its limitations, as I have to be mindful of how much I consume and how fast and who prepared it. If any of those variables don't line up perfectly, I am sick for days. My body and I are at an impasse. It's a lifelong dissension that took a lifetime to reach. Nothing happens without consequence.

MELISSA GRUNOW

THINGS TO END A MARRIAGE

*"Everything that irritates us about others
can lead us to an understanding of ourselves."*
—CARL JUNG

Things he lost:
- His paycheck. ("It will turn up.")
- Work boots. ("I'm not worried. They hurt my ankles, and I can't have steel-toed boots on the construction site anyway.")
- Water bottle for running with his credit card and driver's license in the zippered pocket. (This one was my fault. I was so tired after our 10K on Thanksgiving morning that I don't remember much of what happened before dinner at my sister's house.)
- Eye glasses before an early 5K race. (We later found them on the floor in the living room where he wandered at some point in the night, sunk into the couch, and then crept back into the bedroom before dawn without me—or him—knowing. He did that sometimes. Sometimes, it was hard to keep track of him at night.)
- Trumpet. (Well, more like forgotten, not lost. Maybe it was lost at one time or he thought it was tucked away in a basement behind boxes of old baseball cards, not stuffed inside a closet, nestled between speakers and old shoes,

the worn brown leather of the case barely visible in the shadows of clutter.)

- His keys. ("Can I take your car instead?")
- His passport.
- Checkbook the night before his State of Michigan tax payment was due. ("Did you move it?" Not this time. And this time, I'm not going to help you look for it, either.)

Things I found:

- Love letters to an ex-girlfriend. (Multiple drafts, in fact, or photocopies of the same pages, rewritten paragraphs, coming to terms with the end of one relationship and the start of another. The first woman who didn't love him enough to keep him to herself, the second woman—the letter's intended recipient—who simply decided one day that she just didn't love him at all. His writing is large and loopy in one draft, small and scripted in another, fluctuating between child-like enthusiasm for budding love and passive, matured restraint.)
- A list of women's names written on a 3×5 index card. (Mostly names. Some only descriptions. Two circled together with "3some" written next to them. His "list" was an actual list. "It's not *that* list, just a list. A list of people—I don't know—of women who, you know, I just connected with or wanted to or thought about. It's just a list of women I've thought about. Are you mad? Please don't be mad. You can throw it away. Throw it away if it makes you happy. I just want you to be happy." Never, "I don't owe you an explanation." Because he doesn't, and I can't explain that I want his history to disappear, to go to the curb and never come back.)
- Eye glasses in the shower. ("I had forgotten to take them off.")

- A glass pipe (bowl?) crusted with char, wrapped inside a Tim Horton's muffin bag and tossed in a box along with expired vitamins, a half-empty bottle of mouthwash, an old toothbrush, and a discarded tube of deodorant. ("I didn't know that was in there." Another forgotten item, but not lost, and apparently not missed.)
- 40-ounce plastic bottles of cheap beer stashed everywhere: behind a pile of dirty clothes, in a drawer reserved for pajama pants and sleep shorts, and behind the toilet paper in the bathroom cabinet. ("I wasn't *hiding* them. I was cleaning.")
- Mushrooms wrapped in tinfoil zipped inside a pouch of expired condoms. ("Someone gave those to me for helping them move.")
- Beer bottle caps. On the floor, the dresser, nightstand, countertop, ottoman in the living room, next to the unopened mail on the dining room table, under the oven, on the workbench in the basement, next to the laundry soap on the dryer. ("I'm *collecting* those. I'm going to do something with them. You'll see.")
- Prom pictures tossed in among blank CDs and miscellaneous broken electronics.
- Porn.

Things I discarded:
- Receipts, scraps of paper, some of the love letter drafts, expired coupons, old passport photos, travel brochures, business cards for people he'll never call, flyers for events he will never attend, and the expired condoms.
- Newspapers from weeks, months ago, the creases still deep from being folded for so long. ("I was *going* to read that.")
- Eight extra copies of local magazines featuring an interview with Eminem. ("He's from Detroit, you know.")

- All the empty 40-ounce bottles, some with a little warm beer sloshing in the bottom.
- Bottle caps. ("Please stop throwing these away!" as they were retrieved from the trash bin.)
- A brass lamp with a torn shade.
- A rotary dial telephone.
- Gaudy coffee table damaged by a flood in the garage.
- Scrap cable. ("That's not garbage. I can get money for that.")
- Boxes. *So many empty boxes.*

Things I gave away:
- Set of six gold leaf glasses that had never been used.
- Clothes that didn't fit anymore, clothes he never wore, the pleated denim shorts that went out of style years ago.
- The fuzzy toilet lid cover he bought. ("You're supposed to have one of these. So you have something warm to sit on when you clip your toenails.")
- Multiple copies of DVDs acquired for pennies when he worked at Blockbuster.
- Unwanted gifts he shipped to me after he moved out.

Things he broke:
- Travel mugs. ("Sometimes, things just break," I assure him in the beginning. He apologizes anyway.)
- The lid to the cookie jar where I kept the dog treats.
- My spare car key fob.
- A wine glass.
- The lock on the back door.
- The lamp on the table next to his side of the bed.
- The plaster in the bedroom when he tripped and fell butt-first into the wall. ("I was trying to make the bed because I know you like a made bed.")

Things he forgot when he moved out:
- The plaque I made for him out of 600 bottle caps, though it didn't stop him from collecting more.
- Two years' worth of old tax returns.
- A patio umbrella left lying in the grass.
- His wedding ring.

PART 4
MISUNDERSTOOD

GOOD PERSON

*"Our labour preserves us from three
great evils—weariness, vice, and want."*
—VOLTAIRE, *CANDIDE*

It was late, and the building had already emptied of shuffling
students lugging backpacks and cell phones, their voices a rise
and fall of ambient noise and occasional laughter. A student
had stayed after class to inform me that he would need to leave
thirty minutes early once a week. Another had asked if I could
photocopy the assigned readings for her because she couldn't
afford the textbook. Yet another said she would be in Florida
the week of the midterm exam and could she take it early?

I had just reviewed the course policies in the syllabus
where it was clearly stated that the answer to each of their
requests was a hard no, yet they all looked shocked when I told
them so. Each semester, more and more students seemed to
think of themselves as the exceptional exceptions.

In the hallway, I stepped heavily in my high-heeled shoes,
my gait extending my legs straight from my hips. It's the way
I walk when I am in a hurry, and I was always in a hurry. I
thought I was alone as I swept through the faculty mailroom,
tossing leftover handouts into the recycling bin to lighten the
load of papers weighing heavily on my shoulder before heading out to my car and home for the evening.

It wasn't until then that I noticed there was a woman seated at the conference table. I had seen her earlier that evening pushing the cleaning cart through the hallway. I had nodded then and given her a closed-lip smile as I rushed to class.

She was dozing at the table, her face cradled in her palm, wisps of dark hair pulled lose from the ponytail, elbow tucked in at her side. She opened her eyes and smiled at me when I came in the room, shifting herself awake.

"Hello," I said before opening the supply cabinet and surveying the boxes of pens and stacks of Post-it notes.

"You much hard work," she said with a quiet accent that I couldn't place and smiled again.

She asked me about my family. In the weeks that followed, she remembered that I had a sister and always asked about her and my mother's well-being.

She said I was beautiful, like her granddaughter. "Much hard work," she said again.

Her eyes were dark brown and deep-set, her skin surprisingly smooth. When she told me her son was fifty years old, I imagined my grandmother on my father's fiftieth birthday who looked so much older, who was starting to slow down, just a year away from being diagnosed with leukemia. I asked her where she was from.

"Albania," she said.

I wondered where I will be when I am in my seventies or eighties, what my family will look like, how it will feel to get up and go to work every day, especially on cold, dark winter mornings, and clean up after other people well into the night.

"Oh, you're tired," she cooed, rolling the "r" so gently. "I know it."

Her face settled into her empathy, and I nodded. I could it admit it to her.

"You're a good person," she said.

I didn't feel like a good person. I already felt overwhelmed, overworked, and endlessly scrambling, fighting, to get ahead in some way. Worse yet, I was starting to lose my passion for teaching. The more I gave to my classes and my students, the less I got, and it was starting to make me resentful.

"You much hard work," she repeated.

~

Nick grabbed me by the shoulders and shook me. "Mel!"

It wasn't until I looked up at him that I realized I had been talking. Not talking. *Begging.* Trying to convince him to take me home with him for the night, to let me share his bed, to be a body that I could feel next to mine because I longed for one. I wanted comfort and love and familiarity, and I knew for certain I could get at least one of those needs met by him.

"Mel," he said again as he removed his hands from my shoulders. He lowered the volume of his voice.

I swayed a little and steadied myself, felt the butt of a burnt-down cigarette clasp between my fingers. Had I smoked it? Or had I just held onto it to prolong the conversation, to wait out the chill of the October air as strangers exited the pub and filled in around us before moving as a herd toward their cars?

I flicked it onto the ground and reached toward him for another.

He held a flame up in front of me, so I could lean in, inhale, look away, and then back at him. I was crying, embarrassed that I'd had the nerve to ask him, even more embarrassed that he had turned me down.

"You should kiss me," I had said earlier that night, seated on the same side of a booth in an unknown bar before it filled with people I recognized from college.

He had pulled back a little and shook his head.

It had been years since the last time we had been anything more than friends, and even then what we were was indefinable.

His eyes, while always intense, were less aggressive. "Mel, you're better than this."

Was I, though? More importantly, was that really the reason?

⌒

Aside from *The Odyssey*, I had never read any of the texts on the syllabus for the department's flagship world literature class until I was scheduled to teach it. My concentration in graduate school had been postmodern and contemporary American literature. The only time I had even taken a course like the one I was teaching was as a college sophomore. It was one of the few courses in my major that I scraped by with a C, a fact I wouldn't share with my students.

My class sessions were built around key literary terms, close passage analysis in groups, and presentations of their findings. I would chime in when I had something thoughtful to contribute, but I mostly avoided doing the interpretation work for them. Because the texts were challenging, I would guide them through the key plot points and character developments of the excerpt assigned for that day, frantically scribbling on the white board, the marker squealing in protest by the end of the hour.

When we read *The Aeneid*, I scrawled a raging fire on the board to illustrate the funeral pyre. I turned one of the flames into the blade of a sword, read aloud Dido's last speech:

> *"I shall die un-avenged, but let me die," she cried.*
> *"So, so I joy in travelling into the shadows.*
> *Let the cruel Trojan's eyes drink in this fire, on the deep,*
> *and bear with him the evil omen of my death."*

MELISSA GRUNOW

She had spoken, and in the midst of these words,
her servants saw she had fallen on the blade,
the sword frothed with blood, and her hands were stained.

"What happens here at the end?" I asked.

"She kills herself?" Fred offers, and I nod as I draw a betrayed and abandoned Dido onto the blade of the sword.

"Like in *Romeo and Juliet*?" someone else asks. We were not reading that text, but the students were familiar enough with the story.

The suicide is a similarity, I tell them. But the parallels end there. In *Romeo and Juliet*, they can't bear to be without each other. The ending is an example of dramatic irony. For Dido, her death is tragic. Aeneas still leaves her behind and goes off with his fleet. It is partly her love for him that compels her to suicide, but it is mostly her anger. Dido wouldn't have felt betrayed if Aeneas had stayed, since that would have proved that Aeneas loved her, too.

I repeated Dido's last line. " 'And bear with him the evil omen of my death.' She's cursing him for leaving her," I said. "She's punishing him. Her love is vengeful and full of wrath. While there is grief and longing and despair, it is ultimately her anger that is her undoing. Do you see the difference?"

They nodded, a few writing down the revelation in their notebooks at the mention of my use of the term irony. It was on their vocabulary list that week.

～

"Is it okay that I talk to you about this?" Nick leaned toward me with his shoulders, his folded arms resting on the table.

He had started to tell me about a girl but stopped. Maybe he thought he was talking about himself too much. Maybe he thought I wouldn't want to hear it. Either way, I was startled that he felt he needed to ask permission.

"Of course you can."

He spilled it all. He told me about how after so much time of being non-committal he finally wanted to be with her, but he was afraid that it was too late for them to become more than what was.

He never said it exactly, but she made him feel inadequate. He circled around to his self-perceived flaws, would make a joke, and then move past it without realizing that I hadn't laughed along with him, that I didn't think it was funny for him to question who he was in the context of another woman.

"I deserve it, though," he said. "I mean, kind of." He was referring to her blasé attitude, her distance, her insistence that no, it would not work out between them again because there was no spark left.

Three years ago, their roles had been reversed. She was the vulnerable one; he was the manipulator. Seated in that restaurant, he didn't admit that he loved her. He could never say that, at least not then and not to me. But he was open to the possibility of loving her, and that was as good as love itself.

"People are so complex with their feelings and thoughts and ideas and personalities and their endless search for connection. How can it really be just that?" he asked.

"I don't believe in fate," I said.

"But do you believe in destiny?"

"What's the difference?"

He explained that fate is a compilation of circumstances out of your control. Destiny, on the other hand, is a pre-determined blueprint of what you are meant to do.

I had only known of fate in literature, like in *The Aeneid*, where fate functions as an abstract character, an all-knowing and all-controlling being of force. In fact, the central theme

MELISSA GRUNOW

of *The Aeneid*, I had taught my students, was that fate always wins. Many wrote literary analysis essays seeking out textual examples to support that theme. I didn't have to tell them that I personally disagreed.

We are always seeking our destiny, he said. We're looking for something to give us purpose, to find a way to make sense of the lives we have, the relationships we build, the people we hurt, the reasons we suffer.

"Okay," I said. "So then what is your destiny?"

"Huh," he laughed. "I have no idea. What's yours?"

"No clue," I said.

"Well, that's depressing."

I agreed. I thought back to the night a month prior when I had begged him to show me comfort, and he had refused. He hadn't turned me away for me. He had turned me away for her. Most notably, he had turned me away for himself.

After lunch, I dropped him off before my two-hour drive home. I pulled up in front of his apartment building and put the car in park to say good-bye. He turned to me and gave me a look I hadn't seen in years. His body opened toward me and he flicked his chin upward slightly, just barely noticeable, as if to say, "Yes, I approve of this. I am happy with all of it."

"Let me know," he said. "Next time you're on this side of the state."

"I always do. If you ever want to come over to my side, just let me know. I have plenty of places to sleep." Our geographical distance wasn't burdensome for me, yet to him it was as if we lived worlds apart.

He nodded distantly again, his gaze moving away from me and out the passenger window as though searching for the answer. "I need to do that," he said. "It's been too long."

"All you have to do is ask."

I hugged him twice. Maybe I told him that talking to him, sharing space with him, fills my life with light. I probably said something like that, though it would never be an adequate statement, no matter how many chances I had to say it.

~

My classroom was in the multi-purpose room in a dormitory, one of the many living-learning communities popping up across campus. There were no desks; instead, we sat in a circle on folding chairs. A rolling chalkboard was tucked in the corner that I could retrieve when I needed it, but there would only be a few class periods that we would use it.

The course was called Writing about Reading, and it was essentially a composition class with an instructor-selected novel as the core text. Instead of writing about current events in the context of research, students wrote about topics that connected with the course theme, incorporating examples from the text and their lives as supporting evidence.

As I explained this on the first day, one of the students raised her hand. "What's our course theme?" she asked.

"Love," I said.

Their eyes darted around the circle. Some looked thrilled. Others terrified. Some bored. A few confused. "Like *love* love?"

"What do you mean by *love* love?" I asked, prompting a few chuckles.

"You know, like being *in love*."

"I don't know if I have anything to say about that," a male student said while stretching his legs out in front of him and crossing his arms.

A few more laughs.

"We'll be exploring the spectrum of love: romantic love, familial and parental love, friendship, even love for community. Altruistic love."

MELISSA GRUNOW

I introduced the novel we would read, *The Feast of Love* by Charles Baxter. We read the first two pages aloud together, and I put them in small groups to discuss how they would annotate those first two pages as a demonstration of active reading.

As I reread the book in preparation for the next class, I scribbled thought-provoking questions in the margins to spark discussion and connections between the course theme and the lessons on various literary elements and components of writing.

Despite their initial hesitation, the students felt compelled to share personal experiences with love in writing and in class. They nicknamed our classroom the "Circle of Trust," and even though it was initially a joke, they honored that trust. There were revelatory moments of personal grief and loss of love in their young lives. Sometimes they cried. They consoled each other with hugs and held hands and offers of tissues and pats on the back.

We laughed a lot, especially when the conversations turned to sex in the novel, and they couldn't believe that they were allowed to speak as freely as they did. They were less than a year out of high school, where high-performing and free-thinking were not always equivocal.

About halfway through the semester and the novel, our class discussion of the day's reading assignment was starting to fade when one of the students tossed her dark hair back over her shoulders and said, "What about you, Ms. Grunow?"

"What about me what?"

"What is your love story?"

The silence felt like a funnel cloud spinning at the center of our circle as they waited for me to answer.

"I've only ever known unrequited love," I finally said. "Either I loved someone and he didn't love me back or someone loved me, and I didn't love him as much."

"What about now?"

I smiled and scrunched my nose the way I do when I'm uncomfortable. "No love to speak of at the moment."

Their faces formed new expressions, as though they were seeing me as a person for the first time.

"Anyway, we have about twenty minutes left, so let's do some journaling. Take out your notebooks, and I'll read you the prompt," and just like that, I was their teacher again and they the conscientious students.

On the last day of class, after presentations, course evaluations, and wrap-up discussions, one student lingered as the others filed out of the room to start their summer vacations. He slung his bag over his shoulder and while he headed toward the door he said, "I hope you find the man of your dreams, Ms. Grunow. Because I know he's gotta be looking for you."

—

"I hope I don't sound condescending when I say this," I messaged him, "but I am really proud of the man you have become." I watched the ellipses dance across the bottom of the screen while I waited for his reply.

"I greatly appreciate you saying that. It has been hell fighting past demons and shackles. I'm glad to hear that this new me is beginning to shine through," he said.

"Absolutely. I knew something in you had shifted within a few minutes of seeing you. You were always a good human, even when you didn't do good things. I think you've really come into your own, and I'm just so proud to know you."

I meant it when I wrote it. I also couldn't help but to wonder how long it would last. Had he worked to become a good person because of her? Or had he done it for himself? Was it even conceivable to wonder if, maybe, he could have done it for me?

In world literature class, we read *The Inferno* after *The Aeneid*, and studied Dante's descent into the nine circles of hell with the poet Virgil sent to be his guide by Dante's beloved Beatrice.

Although we had some discussion about the Seven Deadly Sins, the students struggled with putting *The Inferno* in a contemporary context. I drew a Venn diagram on the board, and instructed the students to copy it down. I labeled one of the circles "sin" and the other "crime" and instructed my students to brainstorm with a classmate as many types of sins and crimes that existed in the modern world. If something was considered both—murder, for example—it would go in the overlapping center of the two circles, as long as both people agreed.

I hadn't enough time to adequately prepare for class; I hadn't even finished the pages that they had been assigned to read, let alone prepare anything more than a plot summary to share. Although the grading for the course was minimal with only nine students, the preparation was both time-consuming and daunting. We hadn't even reached midterms yet, and I was already running out of momentum. If I couldn't maintain it, how could they?

I checked my watch and was glad to see I had used up twenty-five minutes of the fifty-minute class with the activity, and we hadn't even discussed their findings yet.

"Okay," I said as the class regrouped. "Let's hear what you came up with."

We went around the room, group by group, until their answers filled the diagram on the board, some even spilling outside the lines of my original drawing. We paused every few minutes to discuss the correct placement of an indiscretion, and got side-tracked when making distinctions between city laws, state laws, and federal laws, and how crimes can be named and defined differently, depending on the jurisdiction and severity.

I checked my watch again. Only fifteen minutes left of class.

To fill more time, I asked them to determine which Circle of Hell the sins and crimes would fall into if *The Inferno* were a modern-day text.

"Just a few left on the list, so don't lose focus," I said when I noticed them getting restless. "Rape is next on the list. What circle of hell would rape fall into?"

The only woman in the class was quick to answer. "Violence," she said, "which is the Seventh Circle of Hell."

I nodded and was ready to move on to the next one when Bryan blurted out, "Wait, wouldn't it be lust?" He didn't include the circle level in his retort. The student most known for skipping the readings, it was unlikely that he knew which was which.

"Why do you think so?" I asked.

"Because it's sex."

"No," I said quickly. Probably a little too quickly. "Rape is a crime of violence and control. It actually doesn't have anything to do with sex."

Everyone looked at Bryan.

I looked at my watch. Three minutes remaining.

"Yeah but," he started. "You can't actually rape someone without having sex with them. Right?"

The eight other students looked down at their desks, the floor, clearly uncomfortable. Only Bryan looked at me.

Two minutes left. I was going to have to answer.

"I'm going to say it again that rape is a crime of violence." My voice betrayed me when I tried to place the emphasis on *violence*. All I could do was speak louder. "Sex, or penetration, is simply the weapon. It's like the gun in a homicide or say a baseball bat used in an assault. It's a tool to carry out the violence."

A few students shuffled their feet, closed their notebooks, unzipped their backpacks.

"We're out of time," I said. "Check the syllabus for the reading due Monday. You'll also have a quiz next week on the next three Cantos."

It wasn't until they left the room and I started to erase the board that I noticed my hands were shaking. For the next few weeks, I dreaded—rather than anticipated—teaching that class.

The evening had grown dark, but I was certain I had parked on the street that forked to the left behind the brewery.

In the shadows of streetlights, nothing looked familiar as I followed the sidewalk, went left at the fork, and continued down two blocks. I saw a white sedan ahead of me, and pressed the unlock button on my key fob. The lights didn't flash, and it wasn't until I was nearly to the door that I realized it wasn't my car. I walked further, only turning around when I got to the overpass, knowing I had gone too far when the sidewalk ended and my open-toed shoes stepped on debris from the passing cars.

I turned around and backtracked. Maybe I had been distracted and walked right past my car because I thought I had parked further away. I stepped off one curb and up onto another until I was back at the brewery.

"Shit," I muttered. I felt lost, even though I wasn't. Not really. I had been there before. Nick's apartment building where I had dropped him off after many Sunday lunches was right across the street. I knew he wasn't home, though. He was at work, and I was killing time. He had told me not to come, that he would probably have to work too late, that he wouldn't be able to see me, but I was stubborn and kept my hotel reservation anyway. "Even if you get out late," I had reasoned, "we could just meet up for lunch tomorrow or something." We were on the phone as I drove from northern Michigan through a sprawling landscape of nothing but fields and trees, the occasional farm in the distance. Cows, goats, and horses grazed or meandered about, unfazed by the noises of the highway.

Nick was still talking, frustrated with the mistakes of his crew. I took that as a sign that he needed to get off the phone, but he said, "Can you talk for a while?"

"Of course," I said, and settled back into the driver's seat, holding the steering wheel with one hand as I repositioned the phone against my ear with the other. "As long as you don't mind that our calls keep getting dropped. I'm pretty much driving through the middle of nowhere."

He assured me it was okay. He didn't get frustrated with me or the limitations of our shared technology in a landscape that hadn't yet caught up with the desired convenience of being able to reach anyone at any time.

"Are you tired?" I asked.

"Nah," he said. "I did a bump right before my shift. I'm good for a while."

I wasn't sure I had heard him. "A bump?"

"Yeah," he said. "You know. Cocaine. It helps get me through these long shifts."

Even though it was warm in the car, I felt a shiver shake along my spine. "Seriously? When did that start?"

"I mean, I don't do it all the time. Just on these long shifts, you know?"

No, I didn't know. With his single admittance, I felt as if I no longer knew him.

He shouted to someone on the other end, a muffled exchange of questions and affirmations. "I gotta go," he said. "I'll text you later."

The phone call replayed in my mind as I headed back up the street, studying each car carefully. I passed by a barbecue joint where people were inside dancing to live music. There was a law firm, closed for the weekend. A glass-blowing studio that looked like it had been closed for a while. Next, a private parking lot with a single chain blocking the entry. Finally, the overpass, the broken glass, the overgrown weeds.

The shoes that I normally wore with pantyhose were rubbing against my heels, my legs bare under a summer dress.

I passed the glass-blowing studio, the law firm, the barbecue joint until I was back on the corner facing the brewery.

I hadn't missed it. My car wasn't there. *It's been stolen,* I thought.

Had it, though? Was it possible I parked on the right fork instead of the left? It was possible I had gotten disoriented, perhaps paying more attention to my phone than my surroundings as I had approached the entrance.

There were no cars parked on the right fork. The whole street was a "no parking" zone. *This isn't right,* I thought.

I was panicked and my cell phone was low on battery. If my phone died, and I died, would they know who to call? During my sophomore year of college, I taped access logins and passwords to the inside door of my bedside table so that if I died, my family could settle my affairs and maybe delve into my files to discover my stories. It was a simultaneous fear and goal that someone would finally know my private life. Even then, would anyone really know me? Would I be remembered as a good person?

I turned around and continued walking, past the barbecue joint, the law firm, the glass-blowing studio, the private parking lot to the overpass and back. In that moment, I was Dante lost in the forest. I had wandered off the one true path and into a fearful place, away from civilization, the freeway overpass at the end of the road much like the Acheron River in *The Inferno*. I sent Nick a text but knew it was unlikely I would hear a response. I shouldn't have been there anyway. He told me not to come. He would not be my Beatrice or my Virgil and so I had no choice but to turn back and try again.

Small gatherings of friends passed me by as they headed to the brewery or back to their cars. They walked with such decisive certainty, laughing and chattering amongst themselves. They stepped around me if I was blocking their path, but otherwise they paid no attention.

I had to call the police. I had to call for a ride. I had to call Nick, though I knew it wouldn't do any good. If he answered, there wasn't anything he would be able to do. If he didn't answer, my heart would break as I knew I had lost him again. Instead, I called no one and kept walking. My shoes continued to dig into my ankles and my dress did very little to keep me warm as the spring day cooled off in the dark. I clutched my keys and pressed the panic alarm on the key fob, but wherever my car was, it remained silent.

It had been an hour. I decided to walk back to the brewery to get my bearings and figure out who to call, maybe find an outlet to charge my phone. I crossed the street, but instead of turning right and continuing down the block toward the door, I cut across a parking lot to the street on the other side.

I was certain I was wasting more time, certain I hadn't even driven down this street, let alone parked on it. Half a block away, I could see the outline of a fire hydrant on the sidewalk. I had driven past one before finding a parking space, so maybe I would just take a look, just one attempt, and then

MELISSA GRUNOW

I would call the police or get a ride back to my hotel or do something to get off the street and out of what was most certainly going to turn into rain.

I saw a white sedan. Maybe it was silver. It probably wasn't my car, I reasoned, but I hit the unlock button on my key fob anyway.

The hazard lights flashed. I pressed the button again, and again the lights flashed.

I had found it. I had found it in a city, on a street, outside a brewery where I shouldn't have been in the first place.

It wasn't until I climbed into the driver's seat that I realized my shoes had torn the flesh away from the back of my feet and stained the grey suede with blood.

I went back to the hotel, took a shower, and fell asleep. I didn't see Nick that night. I didn't try to call him the next morning. He was headed down his own dark road again, and this time I couldn't follow him. Maybe he would make his way back to me; he always had before. For now, though, whatever there could have been with him had passed. I didn't have to understand it. I just had to accept it.

⌢

It was the third week of class and the third week in a row that Brittany had ticked off a list on her fingertips of the reasons why she couldn't do the assignment, read the textbook, or draft the essay. Tonight's issue had something to do with her printer, how she didn't have a print card to use in the library, and she wasn't about the pay the fee to take out cash from the ATM to get one.

"You seem to know what your choices are," I said. "Yet, you still chose to show up unprepared."

I watched her spirit break across her face like a page turning. "I can't discuss this now," I said. "I need to start class in a minute."

For two hours I went through the motions of teaching, feigning enthusiasm for thesis statements and topic sentences. I covered the board with hastily scribbled Venn diagrams, asking for contributions from the class to illustrate how to effectively compare and contrast two topics. While many in the class shouted answers or asked questions, Brittany sat quietly at her desk with her arms crossed.

I tried to shrug off her attitude while still making eye contact to encourage some kind of participation, but even after the building emptied—Brittany the first to bolt from the room—our interaction weighed on me.

I left the classroom, turning off the light and locking the door on my way out.

The Albanian woman was in the hallway, pushing a yellow cart stacked with cleaning supplies and trash bags. I hadn't seen her in a few weeks, and I missed our interactions.

"Oh, you're tired," she said, smiling her warm smile. She was heading toward the door, and I held it open for her so she could push the cart through.

I *was* tired. Tired of driving, standing, grading, and working a part-time job before going to work in the morning and back at the same part-time job in the evening. I was tired of traffic and freeways and gas prices and dead bugs splattered on my windshield, and paying for oil changes and uncomfortable chairs in waiting rooms that stunk of rubber for two hours just to get my tires rotated. I was tired of trying to get ahead financially and professionally, yet never quite having stability in my bank account or my schedule. I was tired of the time I gave to my classes and tired of ever-increasing demands on my energy. I was tired of appearing outwardly strong and driven and inwardly dissolving into a mess of a person unrecognizable to me.

"You much hard work," she said and clasped my hands.

"You work even harder," I said.

She smiled again, her eyes closing with her long nods.

"Well, have a nice night." I turned and headed toward the parking lot, my heels clicking against the concrete and echoing off the brick buildings.

I worked on that campus for another two years, but I never saw her again. My courses switched from late evening to early morning, and she must have stayed on the night shift. I never learned her name. Had I been a better person, I probably would have thought to ask.

LADY: A RUMINATION

Lady (ˈlādē): noun **lady**; *plural noun:* **ladies**; *noun:* **one's lady**; *plural noun:* **one's ladies**; *noun:* **Ladies**; *plural noun:* **the Ladies**

1. *a woman (used as a polite or old-fashioned form of reference).*
   Synonyms:
   woman, female;
   informal *dame;*
   derogatory *broad;*
   literary *maid, damsel;*
   archaic *wench*

"Cross your legs," my dad's girlfriend insisted. "Nice girls don't sit like that."

Nice girls. I wouldn't know because my mother never explained to me there were different kinds of girls, but I was eight, and I would learn quickly the importance of keeping my knees together, even when I wasn't sitting.

I felt my skin suction in the heat as I complied. I wanted to listen, to be a nice girl, even if it meant discomfort. Being a nice girl was a precursor to being a lady, she said.

I desired to be a girl. I desired to grow into a woman.

I never desired to be a lady.

The woman behind the counter at the Jewish deli where I stopped to pick up bagels and cream cheese for a Sunday brunch complimented my hair.

"Oh," she said. "The color is so pretty! You must be Irish."

I was used to comments like hers by then as strangers—everyone from hairdressers to teachers to women behind me at the grocery store to men in bars—have always honed in on my hair color as long as I could remember. As a child, I would blush and skip away, but I couldn't do that as an adult.

"I'm French, actually," I said, smiling. As a woman, I knew it was best to always smile when correcting people.

"But your face—it's so *round*. The French have thin, *thin* faces." She traced the shape of her own cheek with her hand.

My face, like the rest of my body, particularly my thighs, my butt, and even my belly were thick and round. I didn't know how to explain the dichotomy to her; instead, I was instantly defensive. How was she to know the shame I carried inside my weight, my mother's lineage and my father's genetics wrestling endlessly within my DNA? While I longed for my mother's small frame and freckled skin that never burned, it was my father's ambition, work ethic, and problem-solving that I embodied the most.

A handful of men in my life have called me Mel almost as soon as they knew me. I'm reduced to play the role of a sister or one of the guys. They are the men who have never thought of me as a woman of desire. The nickname was a bifurcation, a way to split my identity and femininity. To them I am Mel because Melissa is too lady-like. My command of a room, propensity for swearing, and declarative statements without hedging defeminize me. These men have never known me to cry.

Professionally, I'm Melissa, more so out of habit than desire. On the phone, some think I'm saying "Martha" when I introduce myself which makes me question how well I enunciate and how well they listen. Others hear my name and call me "Michelle" by mistake. My name sounds nothing like Michelle. My name sounds nothing like Martha.

When I was ten, I looked up my name in a book I found in the library. Hoping my name meant something strong like "warrior" or beautiful like "princess," I was more than disappointed to learn that it meant "honey bee." *How stupid,* I thought. *Everyone hates bees.*

"How did you choose my name?" I asked my mother when I was sixteen, just two years away from the age she was when she got pregnant with me.

"We used our yearbook." She told me they avoided names of anyone she disliked, fat girls, and sluts. There were only a few options left.

"What about my middle name?"

She didn't have an answer. The origin of my middle name remained a mystery for years. I only heard it when I was in trouble and my mother would snarl, "Melissa *LeeAnne!*" It was bad enough that we lived in a trailer park. Did I really need to embody my environment? It wasn't until college that I learned it's actually spelled Le Ann. My driver's license runs the name together in all caps, but it's two different words on my birth certificate and passport.

In the baby name books, my middle name doesn't have its own meaning. It's nothing more than a variation of Anne, simply derivative.

My mother was long gone from my life when I finally admitted that I hated my middle name. "I think I'm just going to get rid of it," I said.

"But I picked it," my dad said. No wonder my mother hadn't been able to give me an answer all those years ago. If any topic had anything to do with my father, she refused to talk about it.

"I didn't know that," was all I could say. Much like my round face and my thick thighs, my middle name was something my father had given to me that was exclusively mine. In the end, I kept Le Ann.

2. *a woman of superior social position, especially one of noble birth.*
Synonyms:
noblewoman, duchess, countess, peeress, baroness;
archaic gentlewoman

Walking through the mall among consumers lugging stuffed shopping bags was a thin man dressed in a pencil skirt and floral cardigan with long stringy hair and an alert countenance.

"Oh my," I heard my stepmom gasp as she sidestepped this man who was so obviously a man, yet he was dressed as a woman.

He caught my attention, too, because he hadn't tried to hide his masculinity. Although he—she?—was dressed as a woman, she looked nothing like a lady.

In comparison, I had the advantage to have already been born female, and I identified as a woman no matter how I dressed. I didn't have to overcome presumptive physical features while I painted on my femininity and puckered my lips just to win an argument, even though my legs spread apart when I sat down, and if standing, my palm rested forever on my cocked hip. I take up space as a woman, rather than crushing myself to suit some definition of a lady. Consequently, I'm unapproachable.

My sister would often say to me, "You're not, you know, a *girly* girl." I nodded but inwardly balked at her statement. *She* rarely wore makeup. *She* pulled her hair back instead of styling it, but because I found dresses to be a nuisance, because I preferred power tools to sewing machines, because I wanted intelligence and creativity to source my success rather than behaving the right kind of way to meet the right kind of man so that I would have the right kind of life, because of all that, I was somehow falling short of my role as a girl, as a woman, as a *lady*.

I thought back to that shopper in the gray skirt, the lop-sided wig. How he—how *she*—looked me dead in the eye and challenged me to challenge our presumptions of her gender identity, knowing she wasn't challenging my attire. I had never been comfortable wearing dresses of my own, but I always took note of how many literal doors were pulled open for me, how many men smiled, when I did.

3. **dated:** *a man's wife.*
   a woman with whom a man is romantically or sexually involved.
   historical: *a woman to whom a man, especially a knight, is chivalrously devoted.*

After I got married the first time, I assumed an ethnicity that didn't belong to me when I adopted my husband's Latino surname. Although the initial name change process was straightforward, I found it tedious and distracting. While I waited in line at the Social Security Office and the DMV, while I drafted letters and made phone calls to my credit card and student loans, my husband's life continued on uninterrupted. He wrote poems, and I filled out forms. He studied for the GRE, and I waited in line for my number to be called.

I had gone through school correcting the pronunciation of my last name. When I made appointments or placed take-out orders, I spelled it out slowly, and more often than not,

MELISSA GRUNOW

it was written down wrong anyway. After I was married, we moved to New Mexico and my last name was suddenly easy and memorable. It was also far too common for me to ever get comfortable. When I searched my name on the Internet, I found there were thousands of us compared to just the five or six who shared my first and maiden name. With my husband's last name, I felt like a fraud, my identity forever relinquished to someone who gave up nothing to be married to me.

When I got divorced, I went through the name change process again, finding it much more problematic than when I got married. While my marriage license was sufficient to change my name the first time, divorce papers, driver's license, and birth certificate were not acceptable. I needed another form of ID, the woman behind the counter insisted. I didn't have a passport then. I needed something else with my maiden name on it. "Like your marriage license," she said.

I had already waited two hours to process the paperwork. My marriage license was stuck in a filing cabinet in my new apartment.

I was twenty-five and starting my life over, having no idea what that life would look like. Without a new Social Security card, I couldn't change my license, my credit cards, even my lease.

"Can you accept *anything* else?" I pleaded, pulling card after card out of my wallet and laying them out on the counter.

She pointed to a piece of paper listing all of the documents. I shoved it away. I had the list memorized. I found it on their website, but it wasn't clear that reverting my name to what I had been given at birth would involve so much more than assuming an identity that never felt like it belonged to me.

"I have my birth certificate," I said. "I have three other forms of identification on that list."

"Your birth certificate is proof of life," she said. "Not proof of identity. You need your marriage license."

"So what you're saying," I started, my throat tightening around my frustrated tears, "is that I have an identity as a married woman but not as a single one?"

She shrugged and her eyes rolled to the growing line in the lobby behind me.

I felt my face turn red as rage bubbled in my gut. I could scream at her. I could cry. I could insist on speaking to a manager. I could do all of those things, but I knew they would get me nowhere. I knew she dealt with difficult people all day, people who hadn't read the rules and didn't come prepared. But those people were not me. I had prepared the best I knew how, and still it was futile.

"Okay," I finally said. "Fine." I shook my head to toss my hair back over my shoulders and stood up straight as I gathered the cards and papers I had spread out over the counter. Although I could feel my anger express itself in my face, I couldn't bring myself to be rude.

Instead, I turned away without thanking her and stomped toward the door, the heels of my shoes clicking loudly against the tile floor.

DOUBLE LIVES

*"I learned to recognize the thorough and primitive duality
of man; I saw that, of the two natures that contended in
the field of my consciousness, even if I could rightly be said
to be either, it was only because I was radically both."*
—ROBERT LOUIS STEVENSON,
THE STRANGE CASE OF DR. JEKYLL AND MR. HYDE

Darkness pushes dusk aside and settles quietly. I avoid my
reflection in the window as I scoop ice cream into a bowl.
Using the back of the spoon, I smash it down to make room
for more. There is one bowl in the cupboard that is larger than
the rest, and it's the one I use solely for ice cream. On days like
this one, I can fit half a gallon of Moosetracks into the bowl if
I scoop strategically and intentionally.

It's barely 7:30 p.m., yet I'm already donning flannel pajamas. Today was one of those rare days where I was home even
before I typically left work and crawled along the freeway for
an hour surrounded on all sides by other slow-moving cars. By
slipping out early, I was home in less than thirty minutes, all
ambition for a productive evening gone by the time I closed
and locked the entry door behind me.

I hear my roommate struggling with his key in the side
door. The lock has always been sticky, but it's grown even more
particular since he's moved in. He's hard on things, I notice. He

likes to suspend himself from the molding over the doorways, or rest his weight on surfaces not intended to support an adult man. Normally, if I was standing right next to the door like I am tonight, I would reach over and flip the lock then open it, greeting him with a nod, maybe a smile.

Tonight is different. I'm hoping I can finish filling the bowl, return the container to the freezer, and bolt upstairs before the key finally turns in the lock. I'm just closing the freezer door when he comes barreling in.

"Oh, hey," he says, his voice always upbeat and engaging.

I'm friendly in response, but not too friendly. I can't will myself to endure a round of pleasantries or small talk. I feel badly about it but it doesn't change my behavior. He's always nice to me, always cordial when he arrives home. He asks me questions that I resist answering because talking is stifling. When I finally do mutter a response, the tone of my voice is annoyed and degrading. He doesn't notice or doesn't care. Instead, he goes about his business tossing his bag onto a chair and sifting through a small stack of envelopes on the counter addressed to him.

"Pajamas already?" he asks.

I draw in a slow steady breath and nod. "I'm tired," I say. "Hope to fall asleep early." I'm not actually tired. Not in the way that I imply. I'm exhausted in a different kind of way, as though there is a fog or a darkness in my mind that I cannot shake.

He nods without really listening. "That's a big bowl of ice cream."

I don't tell him it's my dinner. I haven't bought new groceries or planned meals in weeks. Instead, I subsist on Snickers bars and bottled caffeine purchased at 150 percent mark-up from the school store. It seems I'm always in there scanning the stock of junk food at the same time the student in my creative writing class is working the register. We have a silent agreement going: I take a long time to decide on my purchase even though it's the same every day, and he pretends that he's surprised and happy to see me and graciously accepts the $4.28 that I hand over the counter to him. His greetings are accessorized with a smile, but otherwise he doesn't chat with me unless I chat with him. Every transaction ends with, "Have a nice day, Ms. G. See you in class," before I smile back, turn away, and walk out, the heels of my shoes clicking heavily against the tile.

My roommate could stand to take a lesson or two from that student. Sometimes I feel compelled to remind him that his rent only covers his bedroom and unlimited Internet, not the right to judge me or ask questions about my life choices.

Upstairs, there is a *19 Kids and Counting* marathon on my bedroom television. I'm in a race against the commercials, and though I've seen the episode before, I don't want to miss anything. Besides, ice cream melts fast, and I don't want to be stuck with a bowl of something that could best be described as cream soup.

Staying focused on my goal, I slop upstairs when my roommate takes his mail to his bedroom. I settle into bed and turn on the electric blanket to warm my cold toes and prop the bowl up just beneath my chin. A commercial ends, and the show is back on. *Excellent timing*, I think as I wrap my lips around the spoon and savor the cold sweetness as it rests and then melts onto my tongue.

⁓

I made sure I always found a way to slip it into a conversation. "I don't have television," I would say and wait for the other person's reaction. Most of the time it was simply raised eyebrows or a thoughtful nod. Often, I would be met with backpedaling and apologies. "I mean, I don't watch *that* much TV," they would say and then go on to explain why they dedicated time each week to *Six Feet Under* or *24* or *LOST* or *Alias* or some other dramedy or sitcom that maybe I had heard of but probably not. Finding that we would then have nothing to talk about, these closeted television lovers would slink away and talk to someone else who was somewhat clued in to pop culture.

Most of the time, I was met with doubt. "What do you *do* if you don't have a TV?"

I would act sly and smile into the neck of my Zima or gloat that I spent all my time working or reading or doing homework, and that I didn't have time for TV, so what was the point? "I read," I would say. "I read *a lot*. Even for an English major."

However, my statement wasn't entirely true. I did, in fact, own a television. I kept it in my bedroom and ran a cable from the living room, tacking it in along the ceiling in the hallway, and tucked it under the thin gap between the bottom of my door and the weathered carpeting. That semester my TV was always on, and I would spend hours propped up in my bed, a textbook, on my lap and stare at the images flashing in front of me. I would fall asleep with the TV on and wake up to an enthusiastic infomercial or an unrecognizable rerun with commercial interludes advertising phone sex hotlines, luring in insomniacs with lipstick-thick mouths crooning, "Choose me," and smirking at the camera.

Sometimes I wouldn't wake up until the next day when the early morning news programs had morphed into mid-morning talk shows which meant I was late for class again. Before the end of the semester, I had dropped two classes and still barely pulled a "D" in anthropology, a "C" in creative writing, and a smattering of "B's" in my journalism classes, the worst grades I had ever earned.

At the end of the school year, I moved into a different apartment in the same complex, and the TV went in the living room where it stayed for two years. The first year I had a roommate who was rarely home, and the second year I lived in that two-bedroom place by myself because the landlord liked that I paid rent on time and cut me a deal so I could afford it. I found living alone to be both purely joyful and utterly lonely and often fell asleep on the couch or in the recliner chair with a dog-eared copy of *Middlemarch* on the table next to me.

Although I owned a physical television, it wasn't connected to anything but a VCR, partly to save money and partly to prevent me from repeating my academic performance of my sophomore year. Next to the TV stood a small shelf stocked with second-hand movies bought in bulk from video stores. When I told people I didn't have television, I really meant that I didn't have a means of viewing TV shows or the news, and therefore, probably had no idea what they were talking about when they referenced a popular episode or a funny commercial.

Instead, when I came home after class or after work or settled in with a quick bowl of pasta for dinner, I would pop a video into the VCR and watch it for ten minutes, thirty minutes, or its duration, the fatigue of the day sinking me deeper into the couch.

I rarely went out that year. When I did, I settled into armchairs at parties or booths at a bar and proclaimed to be a technology-adverse intellectual bookworm who hadn't yet acquired the taste for beer. If I drank at parties, it was face-puckering malt liquors. At bars, I stuck to Diet Coke and put my energy into cracking the free peanuts and discarding the shells onto the floor and attempted to have meaningful conversation with whoever happened to be sitting across from me.

At home, I was a sweat pants-wearing, takeout-ordering glutton who watched and rewatched such campy flicks as *Major Payne* and *Starship Troopers*. I could have actually used that time to read the books that filled my shelves or write the essays I had been assigned. Sometimes I did. Sometimes, I had a week's worth of homework done by 2 a.m. on Saturday and would finally go to bed when I heard the neighbors return home from their night out. Most times, though, I sat in the dark, my eyes on the television that I claimed not to own.

Living alone gave me the freedom to experience that dual life.

⁓

During another commercial, I change the channel. It isn't until I watch a few minutes of the home shopping network's miracle steam cleaner that I notice the dust that has accumulated in the room around me. For a minute, I consider ripping out the carpeting and refinishing the hardwood floors underneath, even though they squeak and groan under every step I take. I consider vacuuming instead, but the vacuum is heavy and the stairs are steep, and so I put it off until tomorrow, maybe the day after, maybe the weekend.

I flip back to TLC and finish the bowl of ice cream.

Michelle Duggar is explaining something about how her family actually subverts gender roles. Today they are going to prove it by filming an episode for all of America where the girls help Jim Bob work on a car engine and the boys help Michelle with the laundry and preparing a tater tot casserole for lunch.

Their meal choices have always caused my head to tilt a little to one side because they eat a lot of heavy foods: meat and potatoes, fried something or other, sauce-covered noodles, and anything else that can be prepared in bulk and served in a jiffy.

How are they all so skinny? I wonder. Even Michelle, who has spent the better part of two decades pregnant, appears to be a healthy weight despite the loose-fitting shirts that she wears whether she is pregnant or not.

The boys mill about the laundry room, helping Michelle sort giant mounds of dirty clothes into smaller mounds of dirty clothes. They pack those piles into their three expensive front-load washing machines. When the buzzer dings, they transfer the wet piles to the dryers, and then finally, they sort the clothes and hang them by gender and size in the dressing rooms. None of the Duggars have their own clothes stuffed into closets in their shared bedrooms. Instead, they shop off the rack every day at their family-sized walk-in closet. If it fits and is age-appropriate, they wear it. The girls don't cling to a favorite sweater, and the boys don't dig through piles of folded T-shirts looking for their own. There is no fighting, bickering, or arguing over any possession because there is no sense of ownership.

In the garage, the girls look uncomfortable in their smocks worn over long skirts. Jim Bob walks them through how to check the car's fluids, change its oil, and replace a tire. They smile a lot, the girls, but they aren't happy. They look to each other with eyes widened in desperation. They know, or at least they hope, that they will marry a man just like their daddy and that man will know how to do all these things for them. They won't have to worry about grit under their nails or keeping their long hair out of the engine, or wearing something masculine to protect their modest femininity. That man, whoever he is, will fix the cars, chop down the dead trees, build the barn, cut the grass, and figure out why the garbage disposal keeps jamming. That man will solve those mysteries long before they become cause for anxiety. That man will be just like their dad or their admired eldest brother, Josh.

～

We didn't have cable for most of my childhood. I remember a square box against the room with a dial and giant antenna my dad called "rabbit ears" that often had remnants of twisted tinfoil added on in hopes of just a little less snow and a little more clarity.

My perception of the world outside my trailer door was informed most by *The Muppet Babies* and *Punky Brewster*. It was an episode of *The Muppet Babies* that inspired me to write my first newspaper until I realized how many words I needed to generate just to fill a single page. My shaky all-caps print was a limitation, not an asset, as I quickly learned I couldn't write in a straight line, that I had never scribbled more than a few sentences or a paragraph, though I didn't actually know how to recognize a paragraph. I just knew I liked stories and my dad read the newspaper every Sunday, so maybe if my stories were good enough, someone would read them.

Punky Brewster aired on Sundays and her outfits often inspired my school clothes on Mondays, though my fashion attempts were quickly shot down by my mother. A heavy knit dress with thick tights would initially include a read sock over the left leg and a bandana tied at the knee. I would simultaneously mope and strut around the trailer, my cheap Mary Janes quieted by the dark brown carpeting. Mom would be in the kitchen sipping coffee and puffing on her morning cigarette. It would still be dark outside, though frost would gather around the edges of the window, dulling my reflection. In a year, I would sit with my face to that dark window and wait for the baby-sitter to arrive, my mother long gone, my dad a single parent. My morning routine would no longer be monitored by caffeine-guzzling apparition of maternal dictatorship. Instead, I could slip out the door adorned with a quirky mix of layered fabrics, my hair in frizzy pigtails, and brace myself for the gasps of admiration and compliments that would surely come my way as I moved through the crowded hallways to my classroom.

Instead, nobody noticed my daring attire. Nobody seemed to be impressed with my new-found moral code. Punky taught me that if I cheated on a test I would raise suspicion and eventually get caught, puberty is rarely fatal, and to never play hide-n-seek inside a refrigerator. I simultaneously empathized with and envied the resourceful orphaned girl who managed to survive on her own and care for her dog. Even after Henry adopted her, Punky had the treehouse in the courtyard of the apartment building to escape to with her friends and talk through the things they could never convey to the adults in their lives. The treehouse gave them a place to grow their busts, pray for their periods, and to just say no to drugs. By the time any of those adolescent rites of passage were presented to me, the Punky Power lessons had been extinguished long before I had to make those kinds of decisions for myself.

At the time, however, it was Punky's independence that inspired me to fold pajamas, a change of clothes, and my favorite books into a red canvas duffle bag and wait until after dinner but before bedtime to say to my mom, "I'm going to leave for a little while." My voice was quiet while I sat on my bed among my stuffed animals and looked around my room with nostalgic wonder, unsure of when I would ever see it again.

"Where are you going?"

"I don't know," I said. My voice was quiet and serious as I considered her question carefully. I knew what streets to take to get out of the trailer park, and I knew that if it was better to turn right at the busy road, not left, because right would lead me to more people and left would only take me into the country. I hadn't yet decided if I was going to walk or ride my bike. It would be faster to get to this unknown place on my bike, but if I walked, I would have more time to consider my options and would never have to worry about my bike getting stolen. Punky traveled on foot, so it seemed best that I should, too.

"You mean you're running away?" Mom asked.

"I think so."

"You can't run away," she said. I expected her to fess up and explain that she and Dad would miss me, that I was important to the family, that they loved me and would be hurt if I left. Instead, she said, "It's against the law for kids to run away. If you get caught by the police, you will go to jail."

Jail. Even at seven years old, there was no place in the world that I feared more. I didn't want to go to *jail*. Going to jail would be even worse than being at home because I would never be able to leave. I would have to live there forever with bad people who had done bad things. Bad people scared me. Getting in trouble scared me even more.

At the time, I felt endless gratitude for Mom's warning. She had moments like that, moments of warmth where she leveled with me like I was a grown-up. She would share with me some secretive truth, and I would nod along knowingly, appreciative that she would disclose such wisdom to me. I often kept these nuggets of insight to myself, remaining quiet at the bus stop and on the way to school while my friends chattered on about their newest Sweet Secrets dolls or Cabbage Patch kid. Their toys were instantly superficial to me. They didn't know what I knew. They didn't know that kids could end up in jail just for living on their own. While Punky

Brewster taught me a lot about life, Mom always found a way to put it into perspective.

———

Jim Bob and Michelle call each other "Mama" and "Daddy," a habit I find both endearing and unsettling. In this episode, they want to get pregnant again, though Michelle's doctor is concerned about her age having an impact on the baby's survival. She nods along with his explanation, her eyes distant until the doctor switches his rhetoric from "nature" to "God's plan." Instantly, she and Jim Bob perk up, look at each other lovingly and smile at the doctor, even though he is telling her another pregnancy could result in stillbirth or potentially end her life.

How easy it is for them to halt their worry the minute God is brought into the conversation. Their blind faith unhinges me, but it also gives me pause long enough to wonder if maybe I'm doing something wrong in my life. Michelle may have sacrificed her body to her husband and the perpetuation of her family, but I have seen every episode—some multiple times—and she has never faltered. She homeschools her children, limits and monitors their access to television and the Internet, lives piously even though she is a millionaire, and she always looks well-rested, optimistic, and *happy*. She is surrounded by nearly two dozen people every day, and her voice always sounds like a Disney princess on the verge of breaking out into song. I get annoyed when my roommate asks about my pajamas, but Michelle Duggar is never annoyed, never discouraged, as long as there is the possibility that she could have just one more baby, or as they call it, "a blessing from God." Her contentment can't help but to make anyone wonder if maybe their unconventional approach to faith, life, and family isn't so unbecoming after all.

Meanwhile, I'm alone in my room, eating ice cream in my bed, and exhausted beyond reproach. I have no patience, no regard for anyone but myself, and I'm decidedly unhappy. I've spent the past twenty years trapped in that place between the glamorization of escape and the serenity of acceptance. There is always somewhere else to be, but there is never anywhere else to go. I long to be something rather than nothing, but I'm waiting rather than living. There is something else here, I think. There has to be. If not, why do I fight so hard? Why do I exhaust myself with the possibility of more, all the while allowing myself less?

—

My fascination with the Duggars had started to wane when the news broke that eldest son Josh had molested five underage girls—including four of his sisters—when he was a teenager. It had been at least a year since I had last watched the show, partly because I no longer had the TLC channel and partly because I couldn't support the family's conservative lobbying against abortion and LGBT rights. Josh Duggar, in particular, had become outspoken about his political morals. A man who was once co-owned a used car dealership in Arkansas with his young wife Anna, whose life decisions had no bearing on anyone but his own family, now held a position with the Family Research Council in Washington, D.C., an organization known to advocate for bigotry in politics. If I had at one time been curious about the Duggars' seemingly traditional family values, that interest was overshadowed by their political involvement.

Like many others, I was shocked by the news of the molestation, though not surprised. I wondered if, at fifteen, he actually understood that what he was doing was not only wrong (which he probably did) but damaging to the girls and maybe even to himself (which he probably didn't). Instead, he had an adolescent curiosity about the female body (healthy, acceptable) and acted on it with the bodies most accessible to him (unhealthy, unacceptable).

I wasn't particularly surprised that it had happened. A "kid-on-kid" abuse scenario happens more than most people, including the parents, ever really know. I have vivid memories of being in early elementary school and a neighbor boy pulling down his shorts to shake his penis at me, laughing maniacally in anticipation of my reaction, which was a mix of feigned disgust and captivation with a body part different from my own.

In Josh Duggar's case, I was surprised that there even had been a police report filed and a feeble attempt at an investigation. I was surprised that someone—probably one of the girls or maybe a sibling who witnessed the abuse—told an adult and that adult told the authorities. I wondered back to my own bad choices as a teenager and the things I did that hurt others for which I never paid a legal price.

In eighth grade I went with my cousin to take care of dogs that she had been hired to feed and let out for a week while her friend's family was on vacation. While she was scooping food into bowls or tossing a ball across the yard, I wandered into her friend's room, opened a dresser drawer, and pulled a wad of cash out of Tootsie Roll bank tucked in snugly against her socks. I pocketed the money and, without a sliver of remorse, joined my cousin outside. The next day we went back, and I found more cash in an envelope on the microwave in an envelope marked "Cathy," which was not my cousin's name, so I knew it wasn't her payment. Altogether, it totaled more than $200.

Having no way to spend it without suspicion, I shoved all the money into the envelope and hid it under a speaker in my bedroom when we returned home from our weekend visit. Later that week, I came home from school to find my bedroom ripped apart, the envelope gone, and parents in the basement, even though my dad shouldn't have been home from work for a few more hours. My cousin called to ask if I knew anything about the stolen money, and I denied it even though I had been caught and the cash recouped.

After the phone call, my parents, too, asked me about the money, and I denied it again. I denied it because I didn't have an explanation for what would compel me to snoop through a stranger's bedroom and take six months' worth of allowance and babysitting earnings that she had planned to use as spending money during a family trip to Hawaii later that year. I didn't get an allowance, even though I did plenty of chores around the house. I didn't get trips to Hawaii or anywhere, really, beyond visiting family in Wisconsin. I was bitterly jealous of my cousin and her siblings because their father was an attorney and they seemed to get everything they wanted.

I wanted something, too, though I wasn't sure what that was. I just wanted more than I had even if that meant taking something from someone else. To me, everyone I knew had abundance. A sum of money lost meant less to them than $200 gained meant to me.

At thirteen, though, I couldn't explain this to my parents. Instead, I sat at the kitchen table and cried. I cried for my envy, I cried because I had been caught, I cried for the embarrassment of knowing the next time I saw my cousins that they would all know that I was both a thief and a liar. I felt a deep sense of shame for my desire for more and perhaps even some shame that my family couldn't give me what I had thought I deserved in the first place.

As I was questioned, though, I stopped denying what I did and said nothing. I sat quietly with my eyes downward, studying the scratches in the wood. I didn't apologize. Not to my parents and not to my cousin the next time I had to spend a Saturday afternoon at a family get-together. I thought that if I said nothing, that if I didn't bring it up, that they would forget and learn to forgive me on their own.

Instead, I waited for my punishment. Grounding was inevitable, but I knew there would be more, and there was. The next day, after school, my mom handed me a stack of lawn refuse bags and told me to dismantle the fence-high compost pile so the dog would stop climbing on it and getting fleas.

I accepted my punishment without a word or an argument. I worked until dark shoveling various stages of decomposition into the tall paper bags and preparing them for curbside pick-up. I didn't stop until there was nothing but a few inches of dirt, yard waste that had already been transformed. I raked the ground until it was level, lined the bags up in the garage, and returned the shovel to its place.

My shoulders and back ached for a week. It was supposed to teach me a lesson, to be a reminder that taking something that didn't belong to me would result in hard work that shouldn't have been my responsibility. Truth is, I didn't mind the work. I felt strong and muscular lifting yard debris out of the pile and accomplished as the pile got smaller and then disappeared altogether. There was effort and then there was outcome. Inwardly, I was proud of the bags at the curb that week. I had been punished, but I hadn't really been taught a lesson.

~

According to reports, Josh Duggar was sent to a work camp for a summer after he was caught molesting his sisters. He wasn't charged with the abuse, just like I hadn't been charged with theft. He wasn't sent to therapy, and neither was

I. Presumably, his victims were given no support or explanation, and neither were mine. In both cases, though, the damage is long-lasting. My friendship with my cousin was destroyed, and I haven't felt comfortable around her parents, my aunt and uncle, since, even though it's been nearly twenty-five years. I never apologized, even though I was—am—sorry.

Since that time, no one has confronted me about stealing that money. It didn't ruin my image or impact the opportunities I've had in my life. When Josh Duggar's molestation was revealed, there was no lying, no denial that it had happened. He publicly apologized, and even though the events happened when he was a minor and long before the Duggars became a household name, TLC cancelled their show and the endorsements they had dried up within months. The day the cancellation went public was the same day Josh's wife Anna gave birth to their fourth child. He resigned from his position with the Family Research Council and returned to Arkansas a shamed perpetrator.

When the Ashley Madison website was hacked, and it was revealed that Josh Duggar had not one—but two—accounts set up to cheat on his pregnant wife, viewers of the show barely flinched. When he admitted to being addicted to pornography, we expected nothing less. Attention turned to his wife Anna who was indirectly criticized by the Duggars for not submitting to her husband enough so that he had to seek sexual gratification elsewhere. She was blamed and shamed and he was sent away, again, this time to a rehabilitation center for treatment while Anna mothered their children in silence and grew closer to the oldest Duggar daughters, a collective of victims. The family image had been tarnished and the Duggar name forever synonymous with hypocrisy.

How we love to watch perfection unravel.

The first time I remember stealing something, I was just five, maybe six. I was trailing behind my mom in the grocery store as she zipped through aisles, tossing items into the cart, and hastily crossing them off her list. It was late, I think, and I was tired, and I was probably whining to go home, that I was hungry. I had on a large, unzipped winter coat and probably a hat. My boots clunked heavily against the industrial grade tile. As I was catching up to my mother, I saw a small candy bar sitting on the ledge of a clothing display. It had clearly been discarded without thought and left out of place among folded sweatshirts and turtlenecks. My right arm jutted out as I passed it, and I scooped it up in my hand then slid it into my coat pocket. I expected my mom to whip around and scold me and tell me to put it back, but she hadn't noticed. Nobody noticed, and the candy stayed securely in my pocket throughout the checkout lane, the cold walk through the parking lot, and all the way until we got home.

That night, I snuck it into the bathroom while everyone was sleeping, unwrapped it, and took a hurried bite, nearly gagging on the coconut and marshmallow filling. It was disgusting, but I ate it anyway because it was the only way to get rid of it. When I was done, I hid the wrapper in layers of toilet paper and shoved it to the bottom of the wastebasket, then snuck back into bed.

In the morning, I could still feel the bits of coconut in my teeth, and there were the slightest remnants of chocolate coating the corners of my mouth. Even then, no one noticed.

For most people, there is a private self within all of us that is too dark or shameful to admit even to those who love us the most. When Josh Duggar apologized for his "inexcusable actions" from when he was a teenager, his wife Anna stood by him. She had known all along, she stated later, at least two years before they had been married. She accepted his past and, in turn, accepted him. She had not known about the Ashley Madison accounts, the infidelity, the alleged sex addiction. Even if she had known, she had no basis on which to understand those things. Her life had been lived for her husband and family. His betrayal revealed that he had been living only for himself. In the darkest recesses of our mind, there is the capacity for profound deception as we attempt to negotiate the contradictory tendencies of our dual selves, and in the process, dredge up shock, humiliation, and even disgust in regards to our perverse nature. We make excuses when we eat ice cream for dinner or lie about watching television because it isn't an intellectual pastime. We can't help but to scoff at and judge someone like Josh Duggar, yet he stays in the media and on our minds because the revelation of his whole self is compelling. We identify with those similarities and are simultaneously ashamed of those same similarities. It's a paradigm we all live with, whether or not we can accept or ever admit it.

MELISSA GRUNOW

WHITE SPIRIT

"Woch nan dlo pa konnen doule woch nan soley."
Translation: A rock in the water does not
know the pain of the rock in the sun.
—HAITIAN PROVERB

I was in a lounge chair next to the pool while my brothers took turns jumping flips off the diving board when my grandma walked out the back door, shuffling her legs forward at the hips. She wore a black-one piece black bathing suit even though Grandma never went in the pool, and she served my dad and my then-boyfriend each a Manhattan. We asked her repeatedly to sit down, insisting that we could get our own refills. But everyone was always a guest in my grandma's house, so she waited on us in her bathing suit as though it were perfectly normal for her to do so.

In a few minutes, I would go inside to help her prepare lunch: cold-cut sandwiches, deviled eggs, chips with French onion dip, tuna salad, and grapes. We would eat on the patio and stay out all afternoon until the mosquitoes chased us inside. I hadn't broken the news to my family yet that I had become a vegetarian, so when it came time to eat, I picked at the food, blamed my fullness on all the snacks served earlier, and waited for Grandma to bring out the watermelon.

It was July, and we were celebrating her eightieth birthday.

In the fall, as my grandpa's physical limitations and Alzheimer's progressed, they would decide—or perhaps Grandma would decide—that they wouldn't drive to Florida for the winter anymore, the first Christmas in as long as I could remember that they stayed in Michigan.

Grandpa wasn't the only one who was changing, however. Grandma's curves straightened out as she thinned down, and we blamed the stress of being the sole caregiver for my grandfather, who was struggling more and more each day with communication and physical mobility.

What she didn't know, what none of us knew, is that she had leukemia.

⁓

The drill head squeals against the misguided screw. There is a collective groan from the men around me who crouch on the ground and hold the metal frame together.

Miguelson pokes his finger into the air and rotates it counter-clockwise.

"Take it out?" I guess as I drag my arm across my forehead to catch the sweat building on my face.

"*Oui*," he says. "Take it out."

I push the reverse mechanism on the drill. The screw pops out and falls to the ground.

Miguelson offers it to me.

I reposition the screw and try again, this time securing the two panels together.

"Good." Miguelson smiles and nods toward the next hole further down the partition as crewmen scramble to line up the holes. I'm among a small group of Americans who are assembling frames for homes that will be relocated to various villages outside of Les Cayes, Haiti, as part of a grant for Port-au-Prince refugees who fled the country's capital after the

2010 earthquake. I'm a white American woman volunteering on a crew of black Haitian men. Somehow I'm holding the drill and leading the project while the other members of my volunteer group have each gone to work on a separate project with a separate crew. I'm sweating through a layer of bug spray, sunscreen, and every piece of fabric I'm wearing while working in a field under Caribbean sun. The men are clad in T-shirts and jeans, and accustomed to working outdoors in the heat. They're sweating, too, but barely.

We're spread out on the grass next to a row of shipping containers on the grounds of Pwoje Espwa, or Project Hope, a village of sorts that grew from an orphanage of 650 abandoned children. Local children attend their elementary and secondary school, and villagers benefit from the giant outdoor kitchen that serves three thousand meals a day. There is also a medical building staffed by Doctors without Borders, wood and metal shops where young men learn skills to earn money for themselves and their families, a small farm, and a guest house called The Quad where volunteers pay a modest fee to eat and sleep for the duration of their stay.

The men on the crew work for Virginia-based Shelter-2Home, an organization that is under contract to build more than thirty houses throughout southern Haiti for those families most in need. The crew is local men trained and paid by Shelter2Home to build these houses, whose frames lock together like giant erector sets, and are then covered with mesh and stucco. The homes are designed to be resistant to severe wind and rain, rot, and infestation, all shelter threats in Haiti.

A bell rings and children dressed in pink and white gingham shirts and green shorts or skirts gather around our work site and watch us. Children in Haiti are required to wear uniforms to school, and the Americans call this particular group the Watermelon Patch because of their attire. The children call us over to them, "Please! Please! Photo! Photo!" they say, those who aren't too shy, at least. I pose for pictures with them, and one girl gets trampled as they scramble around me like puppies, tugging on my clothes and hugging my limbs. They are desperate for affection, and I can't keep up with their desire. When the bell rings again, I pry them from me, point to their school, and shout firmly, *Au revoir!* to direct them back inside.

—

I spent a week with my grandparents when I first moved back to Michigan after graduate school. I didn't have a job yet, so I drove two hours to their house, where I had my own room and I could lounge in the sun by the pool reading books, dipping my feet in the water to keep cool. I looked beyond my toes and saw the drain in the center of the deep end of the pool. When I was younger, I would try to swim all the way to the bottom, the pressure increasing on my skull the lower I sank. I would slowly exhale to get closer and closer to the bottom, and by the time I reached the grate, I would be completely out of air reserve. My cousins and I would play a game to see who could sit cross-legged on the floor of the deep end. Kristin could always do it. I never could. Sitting on the edge of the pool, I wondered what it would be like to get to the bottom and to open my eyes, nose, and mouth, and take in water instead of air. I wondered what it really meant to drown.

When I stopped moving my legs, I could see my reflection in the water. The older I got, the more I looked like my grandmother when she was young.

—

We fly from Detroit to Miami and from Miami to Port-au-Prince, where a hired driver takes us to the Tortug Airport. From there, we are given hand-written boarding passes for a flight to Les Cayes. Our plane sits no more than 18 people and flies so close to the ground that I get to watch the Haitian countryside roll out in front of me. Beyond the mountains, I see more mountains, greenery, and clear water. No evidence of the country's poverty or corruption or great suffering. Just paradise.

A driver meets the six of us volunteer builders—Christine, Margaret, Darryl, Michael, Dominic, and me—at the airport with a car meant to seat four. The ride is scenic, yet cramped and bumpy. Men, women, and children stare as we drive by. The children wave and shout. There are tin shacks that say "bank" on them along the way, but I'm told they are really casino stands for the lottery that is impossible to win. "It's the government's way of ripping off the poor," Christine says. This is her second time in Les Cayes to work with the local construction crew, and she frequently offers factoids about the living conditions and corruption, though we have no way of knowing for sure if they're true.

Judex is a former Espwa orphan who finds out The Quad has visitors. When I speak with him, I don't need to slow down or choose simpler words. His English is self-taught and flawless. He speaks just as I do with a nasally Midwestern American accent and an adult's vocabulary. "It's how I will live," he says of his mastery of the language.

He offers himself as a translator for twenty dollars a day. We decline, hoping to make do for a week of volunteering with one of us speaking broken high school French and the Haitians knowing enough English that we can assemble panels and install doors without compromising the building's integrity. We communicate on grunts and motions and smiles. Everyone is unnaturally polite and patient with us. Haiti is a happy country, and if the crewmen don't want us there, they sure don't let on.

My grandparents came to visit me my first semester in college. After dinner, they took me to the casino where they weren't sure if I needed to be 18 or 21 years old to get in, but we walked right past the security without alerting them enough to check my ID.

Scenes from movies came to life in front of me. The bright colors, the shiny chrome, the unremitting ringing and dinging of slot machines. My grandparents were seasoned gamblers and showed me around the floor. They gave me five dollars and taught me how to play roulette and the slots. I watched as men and women of all ages and health conditions plunked down stacks of bills or piles of chips or fed coin after coin into the machines. I wanted the feeling of success, of gathering my winnings and running out the door, and into the evening light.

I lost the money within minutes and shrugged as my grandpa laughed and reminded me that gambling was just that—a gamble.

"Now, don't tell your parents that we brought you here," Grandma said. She set her lips in a tight line on her face as the flashing lights from a nearby game danced in her eyes. "I don't want to get you into trouble."

On our first day of work, the six of us walk through what can only resemble a jungle from my city-minded perspective, to a two-room house that's already been framed and covered in stucco. We're met by Pierre Claude, a Haitian crew leader, and some of his men, to install entryway doors that are contractor-grade and shipped from the U.S. The house has two entrances and there are more than ten people trying to help install the doors. They don't need me. I stand in the front room and watch, wondering why I'm here and how I'm going to contribute, when a woman hands me her baby through the frameless window.

Pierre Claude turns to me and smiles. "This is her house," he says, nodding to the baby.

"Wellbene," the mother says through gold fillings, pointing to the baby. "Wellbene." The child is quiet in my arms, nearly expressionless unless I make cooing noises, and then she giggles and smiles, the mother smiling, too. I try to ask the men how old she is, but they don't understand my question. That, or they don't know how to answer. The language barrier divides us.

—

As my grandmother's life approached its end, I reached out to Edwin, a man who would never be my boyfriend because he was a bit of a mystic, an overgrown lost boy, a misguided hippie, and a broken-hearted. He teetered on the line between alone and lonely. He was a genius and clueless, a connector who struggled to communicate. He was emotionless and full of emotion, fascinated and disinterested.

Edwin lived in a realm of universal energy, a space of love, truth, and healing, and he tried to get me to live there, too.

"My grandma is dying," I said. I called him from my bedroom in my apartment, face down on the mattress, unsuccessfully trying to cry. We hadn't seen each other or spoken in months, yet he was the only person who could crack me open so that I could mourn.

"Completely surrender yourself to this moment." Edwin's argument was that when you surrender, you're allowing the release of all things you want to control. "Love," he said. "Don't grieve. Just love."

Edwin said he had been in a dark place. That he missed me. That he hadn't met anyone like me since our brief affair had come to an end a few months prior. He said our connection couldn't be matched.

"And plan to stay the night," he said after calling me up and inviting me over for dinner.

I accepted his invitation. I couldn't save my grandma, but I could try to save Edwin.

In the end, I failed them both.

~

"Melissa, there's one next to your head."

I open my eyes, and my ears slowly adjust to the whirring of a large industrial fan propped up in the corner of the room. I'm lying under a screened window and a thin sheet. The fan had cooled the night just enough for me to fall into a sound sleep, despite the heavy humidity in the air.

I fold forward, crawl to the foot of the cot and stand up. It isn't until that moment that I am actually awake enough to realize Margaret, my roommate and fellow volunteer, is standing next to me with a flashlight in one hand and a flip-flop in another. It's our first night in Haiti.

"There's a what next to my head?"

Margaret hands me the flashlight. "Here," she says. "Look. It's on your bag."

My duffle bag is on the floor next to the cot, and sprawled on the side is a giant spider.

"My god," I say. "It's the size of a Frisbee."

~

Grandma couldn't drive anymore, not for long periods of time, anyway. So I called in sick to spend the day driving my grandpa to doctor's appointments, run errands, and buy their groceries. I put gas in their van knowing the tank would likely be just as full on my next visit. I was working two jobs, and for that reason, didn't have time to go up and help, aside from that one day when I hoisted my grandpa in and out of the car, my grandma nagging him the whole time to adjust his shirt, pull up his pants, stand up, sit down, step closer, and don't go too far.

My grandpa died first. A heart attack, Dad told me. Alone in his room, he was found by an orderly at the nursing home where we moved him after my grandma became too weak to care for him. At the funeral, I sat in the fifth row and cried quietly but hard, cousins and siblings piling into the rows around me. I wouldn't look at any of them, just at the floor and at my niece who was too young to know not to laugh, who didn't understand loss. My grandma had told me not to cry, not be sad. She spoke through a white mask while seated in a wheelchair, barely healthy enough to not be lying in a hospital bed. Months later I would wonder why I cried so much at my grandpa's funeral, and not a single tear at my grandma's. No, at her funeral, I half-carried, half-dragged my thin sister to her seat, holding her tightly, knowing her grief had overcome her, wishing I had someone when I was the one who needed to be carried.

⁓

Today is my ten-year wedding anniversary. Or at least it would be if I were still married. Instead, I am five years divorced and in another country while my ex-husband is in Utah doing whatever it is that ex-husbands do.

The volunteers and a few crewmen ride in the back of a pickup truck with two doors propped up between us and speed down a dirt road into a neighboring village. We are headed to a house that will belong to a young woman who lost her leg in the earthquake.

When we arrive, the woman shouts greetings to us in *Kreyol*—Haitian Creole—the crewmen shouting back at her. She hobbles over to us and kisses my face, leaning in on her crutches, as one of the children wraps his arms around my thigh and giggles. Some of the men unload the doors from the pickup truck. A quick measurement tells us that we need to clear the frames of screw heads and additional mesh. We use whatever tools we can find: rocks for hammers and our keys as pliers since there are not enough tools to go around. At one point, I use the bottom of my metal water bottle as a chisel and hit it with a rock. Pierre Claude laughs at me, but the technique works, so he nods and moves on to the other door frame. It's another hot day and one of the crewmen offers to take over for me when I pause to fan my T-shirt out. I'm grateful to have a break.

Children from the village are crowding the crew, so I take them a few yards from the house and teach them hand-clapping games and Ring around the Rosie. One of them is wearing tights for pants, another just a cloth diaper, and another a matching tank top and shorts set that should belong to a young boy, but is worn by a little girl. None of them are wearing shoes except the girl with the tights. When they get bored with clapping and skipping in a circle, they take turns clutching my hands and climbing up the front of my body then flipping backwards, landing on the ground, a game I used to play with my dad in my grandma's pool when I was young.

—

When Grandma was initially diagnosed with leukemia, she was given six months to live. She made it almost two years because it took that long for her body to take over her spirit.

"I'm not afraid to die," she told me once on the telephone as I drove the hour from my day job to my evening job, negotiating traffic and accepting her acceptance. "I just don't want my mind to go first. Don't let that happen, okay? I want to know who I am and where I am at all times."

MELISSA GRUNOW

In the end, her mind stayed sharp, just like she wanted. She contracted pneumonia, fluid built around her heart, and she couldn't get enough oxygen on her own. Her body deflated and drowned itself in a hospital bed, my dad and his siblings by her side.

—

I'm *blan*, or white. A foreigner. There is a Haitian proverb, *Milat pov se neg, eg rich se milat*, which translates to, "A poor mulatto is black, a wealthy black is mulatto." Race and wealth are positively correlated in Haiti. A white woman, an American woman with a fleshy physique like me, is a prize in a crane machine, and the men all seem to line up with a pocket full of quarters.

Judex tells me, "I've always wanted to try white." He's nineteen. I'm approaching thirty. I turn away, embarrassed that he is so brazen.

Michele is a crewman who wants to bed me. "Maleesa," he says to me, my name a magical word in his mouth, "I need you. I need you tonight."

Kevins is a *vakabon*, a former street kid. He often works by himself as the others see him as a hoodlum or a freeloader. He doesn't care. He hugs me tightly and flashes a peace sign when we pose for a picture together.

Fritznel tells Miguelson that he loves me, and Miguelson translates.

I shake my head.

"What?" Miguelson asks. "You don't like black?"

I immediately think of my grandmother who would answer for me in a situation such as this. "I like black just fine," I say. "But I'm going back to America in two days."

Legoute introduces himself to me as Son Son, a common nickname. We talk, smile, even flirt for three days while assembling wall panels together. On the last day I give him a bracelet I had made for him with "Son Son" stitched on it. I show him the one I had made for myself with my own name on it and say, "See? So you will remember me."

He hands me his bracelet back and tugs on the one on my wrist.

"You want to trade?"

He nods. "Your name. On my heart." He gives me his phone number and requests that I call him. "I want to have your words," he says.

They call me a *lespri blan*, or white spirit. "They have never seen a woman work the way you do. They're basically calling you a freak of nature. It's a compliment," their American foreman tells me.

No matter their English skill level, they all ask me the same question, "When will you return to Haiti?" Always when, when, when, because once you have Haiti in your heart, you always will find a way, and a reason, to go back.

⁓

My cousin Heather picked through my grandma's closet after she died and stacked a huge pile of clothes on the bed to take home with her, while her mother—my aunt Carol—sorted through piles of my grandma's jewelry, all of us still dressed in our funeral clothes. I sat in my grandma's bedroom and watched them, wondering how it was so easy for them to collect her belongings for themselves so soon.

My uncle told me to take the Asian-inspired table with the peacock and bamboo stalks painted on it that my grandma promised to me during a conversation while she was sick in the hospital.

"It's that one you said you liked," she had reminded me. "The one we used to have at the house in Florida." It had been twelve years since I said I mentioned liking the table. Twelve years, and she made absolute sure that everyone knew I was to have it when she died. Heather could have the clothes, the TV in the den, and anything else she picked off that day. The table was my grandma's legacy to me.

—

We arrive at Dan's Creek, a resort in Port-Salut, on our last day in Haiti after a week of installing entryway doors and assembling frames for new houses that the local crew will finish on their own. While waiting for our lunch to be served on the outdoor patio we drink Prestige beer and go swimming in the warm ocean; the sun reflects light in all directions for miles. The resort is positioned at the top of a rocky hill, and the only way to get to the water is to climb down stairs and ladders or to jump from a cliff that overhangs the ocean.

Christine and Margaret run and jump in without hesitation, not at all intimidated by the twenty-foot drop. I am worried about rocks and heights, and scared for absolutely no reason. When I finally get the courage to jump, the water hits me hard, and I sink to the bottom, my feet brushing against the gravelly sand, the bandana once covering my hair now floating out to sea. I expel the air from my lungs, air bubbles floating up from my lips, and try to sit at the bottom. The water is too buoyant, and it doesn't let me do more than kneel. I can feel the sun, even on the ocean floor, and the water pressure compresses my body. I linger, I let my lungs plead for a moment, and then I kick my feet, spread the water with my arms above my head, and take in air when I surface. I make my way to the beach to climb the stairs, walk the plank, and jump again.

WE'RE ALL MAD HERE:
A FIELD GUIDE TO FEIGNING SANITY

"'But I don't want to go among mad people,' Alice remarked.
'Oh, you can't help that,' said the Cat:
'we're all mad here. I'm mad. You're mad.'
'How do you know I'm mad?' said Alice.
'You must be,' said the Cat, 'or you wouldn't have come here.'"
—LEWIS CARROLL, *ALICE IN WONDERLAND*

THE REALIZATION

When it finally happens, it will happen quickly, too quickly perhaps, but quickly enough that it will make you wonder what took so long. There were so many incidents pointing to the moment, the realization, that there may be something wrong with you: snippets of childhood when you felt isolated and lonely at family parties; that time as a teenager when you stole a bracelet from a friend's bathroom because you were jealous she had so much and you had so little, so you took it as retribution for her privilege; days when you would scream and scream and scream at your sister the minute your mom left for the grocery store, just because you could, just because it felt so good to be heard; touching lips with boys you didn't really like or touching skin with men you didn't really know under the guise that you were a feminist and you could do what you wanted with whom you wanted; being the last to clock

MELISSA GRUNOW

out at your fast food restaurant job because you could never get the dishes, the floor, the counters, clean enough. Maybe you had a wedding but never really had a marriage because you felt relief, not grief, when your husband made out with a lesbian at your grad school commencement party. Maybe your divorce felt like an accomplishment when it should have been traumatizing, while actual celebratory events made getting out of bed and taking a shower an all-day struggle.

But you endured all those moments. You trudged through adolescence and into adulthood with minimal scarring. You pursue your education so you can become an educator, to inspire the leaders of tomorrow, particularly those with an entrepreneurial spirit and a global view. You want to work toward something meaningful, toward something of validity.

In short: you want to give the impression that you have your shit together.

And so, the night before a big faculty presentation, you find yourself imagining and examining every possible nuance of every possible situation, anticipating every problem, criticism, question, until your mind devours itself and any chance of sleep. It shows in your dry and reddened eyes the next day as you take the floor, leaning against the long table at the front of the room, rather than standing behind it. You don't need a shield. You're not afraid of them.

Be brilliant. Be impressive. Be *memorable*. Be mindful that if your colleagues hate this program and the vote doesn't go your way that it's very likely you will lose your job.

Brevity is the secret to presentation success, so keep it short. At the end, shift your eyes from the back wall to the faces seated in front of you, and stare down your colleagues for the first time since taking the floor. Brace yourself. "Any questions?"

They will stare. Some will have lowered their tense shoulders. Others will have empty faces, mouths agape, eyes that won't make contact with yours. But they will have one thing in common: silence.

When a coworker dressed as a friend confronts you afterward, she will suggest you seek help. Your speedy, incomprehensible presentation, your shaking hands, your muttering and stuttering and lack of poise, lead her to the only logical conclusion: something isn't right.

"But I was just nervous," you will argue because it's your truth. "There's nothing wrong with me."

You're not saying what you want to say: *I'm not crazy. Am I?*

She will shake her head. You can't fake it on your own anymore. You cannot "pass" as one of the stable, one of the sane. The jig is up.

"Okay," you will concede. "Okay."

She will seem satisfied with your answer. "It will be. Okay, I mean. It will be okay."

You will doubt her assurance, and you should. Because once you step over this threshold, you cannot go back.

THE WAITING ROOM

Every waiting room is different, but everyone knows how they work. Show up, sign in (first name and last initial only to protect your privacy), and wait to be buzzed in, let in, or invited back. The décor will vary. One therapist's office may smell of essential oils, play the relaxing sounds of waterfalls and ocean waves, and invite you to take a free pen and journal from a basket resting on the side table. In another, you'll settle into a winged-back chair in the receiving parlor of an 1890s colonial converted to a medical center shared by an ear/nose/

throat doctor, a cardiologist, and a psychiatrist who believes in talk therapy. The house is old and smells like it, the carpeting tired, and the windows sealed shut with lead paint. You will want to arrive early just to sit in that chair, to rest your head against the inside of it, and feel like a queen upon a throne.

In another, there will be a row of office chairs lined up against a wall. They will be uncomfortable and just a little too high to cross your legs and not wide enough to curl your legs underneath you. They are definitely not conducive to reading and they will squish your body into itself, making it difficult for you to breathe.

The best waiting room, though, the best is the one with the sunken red chairs covered in worn leather and lined with shiny brass tacks, the kind of chair you may come across in your grandma's basement. They are the most comfortable, but also the noisiest, so try to sit still while you wait.

You will find magazines around you, of course, but more than magazines you'll see pharmaceutical rep brochures, empowering you to ask your doctor about a new pill they're pushing. There will be posters, flyers, no-postage-required information request cards. You'll see a plastic box labeled "ADHD Support Center" sitting empty on the bottom shelf of a scratched bookcase. You'll think that's not very supportive, and you'll be right. You're clever like that, so go ahead and snicker, just do so quietly.

There are rules, you know, rules of etiquette to follow while waiting among other patients to see this kind of doctor. Make sure you follow them to the letter or risk being perceived as the most nuts person in the room.

RULE #1: DO NOT MAKE EYE CONTACT.

Your eyes are to be shifty and remain focused on the floor, your cell phone, a book, magazine, or stray newspaper, at all times. You can fluctuate between focal points, as long as those eyes of yours never land on the eyes of another.

It's not polite to stare, but you will anyway. The trick is to stare slyly, through brief peripheral glances, reaching up to smooth your eyebrow or brush your hair out of your face if the object of your glance happens to shift in your direction.

The others fascinate you, but you don't want to invite them into your mind. You don't want to acknowledge that you are all in the same room. You have nothing in common, yet you have everything in common because you're all here for the same purpose. You are all—in your own way—crazy.

RULE #2: DO NOT SOCIALIZE.

Scratching whispers will float between companions: a mother and her teenage son, a mother and her adult son, always a mother and someone else, it seems. The only exception is when they are professionals on lunch breaks, crossing panty-hosed legs, a dangling stiletto balancing on a big toe. You will hear the rise and fall of their voices, pick up words, ideas, maybe more, that intrigue you. You may here a joke or a line of sarcasm that makes you want to chuckle and respond.

Do not chuckle and respond. You are not part of their conversation, and you don't want to appear desperate for socialization. Don't be outgoing or even responsive. Don't make small talk. If there is a window, stare out it until your name is called. You are not here to make friends. These are not your people.

RULE #3: DO NOT DO ANYTHING THAT WILL MAKE YOU APPEAR CRAZY.

Your space in that waiting room, the very seat you choose on your first visit, will say more about you than the amount of time you spend with the doctor, whether it be an hour-long diagnosis session or a fifteen-minute meds check. The staff and others in the waiting room will be poised and ready to slap you with a diagnosis the minute you step through the "crazies only" door. Be wary of the following:

Choose the same chair each time? OCD.

Switch between multiple chairs in the same visit? ADD.

Bring something to help pass the time? Social anxiety.

Bring nothing and slouch? Depression.

Fidget nonstop in your chair? ADHD.

Panic when something, anything, changes? Generalized anxiety disorder.

React emotionally to whatever you are reading? Bipolar.

Talk to yourself while compiling a grocery list? Schizophrenia.

Don't be late for your appointment. Don't be early, either. Most importantly, don't show up on the wrong day, sign in, be ignored, then make a scene an hour later when the 17-year-old behind the desk—probably the shrink's neighbor who needed a summer job—tells you that your appointment is actually *next* week, that your doctor isn't even in today, that you'll get a reminder phone call the day before, like always, remember?

There will be anti-role models all around you, so follow their lead on how not to behave. See the woman waiting in the corner? The one who is draped in a sweater, even at the onset of summer? Yes, her. See how her smirk doesn't stop? Not with eye contact. Not after you're taken to the back office and later return to her waiting quietly in that chair. All smiles, all the time, a grinning idiot.

Don't be like her.

Don't be the woman wearing dark sunglasses who wanders back to see the doctor when someone else's name is called. When the doctor points to another patient and says,

"She's next," don't pretend, at first, that you didn't hear him until he grabs you by the elbow and steers you back toward the waiting room. "*She's* next," he will repeat, so that this time you understand him.

Don't, seriously don't, shake his hand and say, "It's okay, Doctor, I love you," then saunter back into the waiting room to stare at the wall, or least look like you're staring at the wall. With your sunglasses on, nobody will be able to know for sure.

You could be the teenage boy whose mom and dad both accompany you to appointments because their constant doting and hovering will assure the entire office staff that you take your ADD medication, but it will also assure that you will be incapable of growing into a responsible adult who can unload the dishwasher or fold laundry on your own without endless nagging from your impatient wife (best case scenario), or your mother when you're still living at home in your thirties (more realistic scenario). Be grateful, at least, that you are the one advocating for your own mental health, that it is not a family affair.

You may be tempted to be that person who wanders back through the crazies only door, and while passing through the waiting room, remarks, "Today must be purple day," then continue out into the hallway and leave it up to everyone else to figure out what exactly "purple day" means. Don't be that person. Instead, be the one who rolls your eyes at that person.

Here's what you should do: show up wearing Burberry. Wear stylish rubber boots over black leggings on rainy days, huddle under a black puffy coat when it's chilly and sit with your legs crossed tightly. When a new patient walks in, look up, smile thinly, make eye contact, but briefly, just briefly. Like that. That's it. You, girl, are doing it right.

THE RECEPTIONIST

She will be called different things by different people. One doctor will call her by her first name (which you will never remember), another doctor will call her, "The girl at the front." Secretary, assistant, medical something-or-other, does it really matter? You will call her the receptionist, even though you don't feel very well-received when you arrive. Learn the difference between empathy, sympathy, and judgment. You will likely encounter all three in the same visit by the person sitting behind the counter. Nevertheless, when you arrive at a new office, be prepared to confront two kinds of receptionists.

There will be those who smile, are too friendly, too quick to highlight your name when you sign in. These are the "have-a-nice-day" receptionists. They're cheerful only because they're grateful they're not crazy. They go home each night, heat up their microwave dinners in their cookie-cutter apartments, and sit on their sane couches, watching their sane televisions. Their lives are simple, uncomplicated, and easy. They will return to work the next day, highlighter poised above the sign-in sheet, taking great joy in sliding the glass divider open then closed, open then closed, because it gives them a clear divider between the "us" and the "them." You are now part of the "them" group. It's time you accept it.

The other kind of receptionist is the one who is openly fearful of and disgusted by your classification as a mental health patient. The glass partition between you two isn't nearly thick enough so she speaks to you with the window closed, and her voice will crawl further and further up her nose each time. She won't even allow you to use her pen to sign the credit card slip.

"Use that one." She will smile a sneering smile and point to a cup holding a single pen with a giant felt flower attached to the top of it.

Clearly, your illness is highly communicable, and lives on pens, door handles, and toilet seats, requiring delousing powder or bleach and latex gloves to prevent infection. She's risking her own mental health by even working there. *Clearly*.

You may be crazy, but she is insane. Yours hurts only you, but hers is criminal, hurting everyone who walks through the door. She is inconvenienced by your questions, and cages herself off from the waiting room. She has even posted a sign on the partition, "Please be seated. Do not tap on the glass," as if you were a patron visiting the zoo, and she an exotic novelty.

You won't talk again until she has to schedule your next appointment, giving you an explanation for each day and time the doctor can't be available to you. You're stuck leaving work early, again, hoping no one notices.

When you show up the following Tuesday, swipe the sign-in pen, so the receptionist has to share hers with the next patient. Twirl it in your fingers and stare her down from your uncomfortable chair, knowing she won't make eye contact. Feel smug. Go ahead, you earned it. Nibble a little on the end, then rip the petals from the top with your teeth and spit them across the empty waiting room. You'll be making a statement, except nobody will be listening. Leave the chewed pen on the side table when you're called in for you appointment. Smile so widely that the doctor will say, "You're feeling better today, I see."

"Much better," you will respond. "Much, much better."

The following week, there will be a new pen in the cup. No flower with felted petals, though, just a blue ballpoint, generic and ordinary.

THE DOCTOR

You will burn through doctors the way a middle school girl burns through crushes.

The first will be your best, even though she's technically an over-educated nurse practitioner. She's the only one who will combine therapy with pills, and always prescribe something established and affordable. But she's forty minutes away and ongoing road construction plus a demanding job will make it impossible to keep your appointments. You'll miss one because you'll be having one of your paralysis days, those days that no matter what the commitment or how great the stakes, you will not be able to will yourself out of bed. It's a by-product of your illness that will cost you $175 in no-show fees. You'll attend fairly regularly after that, then cancel three sessions in a row, and finally stop booking appointments all together. It won't be until after your meds run out and you start having trouble with flat-lining your rage or committing anything new to memory that you will decide to seek out a doctor who is more geographically convenient.

You may think that talking it out will empower you to fix your problems without the crutch of prescription drugs. If so, get a referral to see a therapist, and start meeting weekly. You will be uncomfortable at first. You won't know how to start or what to say or what issues to focus on. Her office will be dark and smell of the cinnamon tea that she always drinks. You will like that your back is to a window and you can hear the rain hit the glass. Despite the cinnamon that makes your eyes water and the unnaturally dim lighting, you will find her office cozy. You'll sink into her deep, heavy couch and hug a throw pillow as if to say, "Bring on the healing!"

She will convince you to try "energy work." She will suggest you get a Vitamin D lamp to brighten your mood. She'll send you home with a device that you clip on your earlobes to sends shockwaves through your body. You won't get more energy, though. You'll get vertigo and nausea, instead. You'll unclip the device, wrap it carefully and zip it back into its carrying case. You drop it off at her office before you next session, unwilling to give it a second try. Dizzy spells are not the solution to your problems.

"Don't make any major life decisions until you get this sorted out." *This* means your disorder, specifically the meds to treat the disorder, meds that are attempting to quiet the chorus of obsessive thoughts and premature emotions that run the gauntlet of your mind. You need a diagnosis; you need answers. You will decide it's time to see a real doctor, not a therapist.

The doctor with the longest wait is the one with the most uncomfortable waiting room chairs and the snottiest recep-tionist. On average, you will wait at least two hours, no matter how early in the day you schedule your appointment. Others will wander in after you and see the doctor first, an injustice you will complain about to the secretary, but to no avail. The doctor will ignore the pileup of crazies in the waiting room, but make a special appearance from behind her office door when the pharmaceutical rep arrives with free coffee, gift cards, office supplies dressed in logos, and a suitcase full of samples.

When it's your turn, the psychiatrist will smile a smug, unwelcoming smirk that seems to say, "Thank you for your money. Please don't cry in front of me today." You will last a month as her patient before you decide to find someone new.

Finally, the waiting room with the red leather chairs belongs to an 80-year-old man who wears his pleated pants high on his waist. His office will be filled high with papers, file folders, old textbooks. On a filing cabinet, he will have a wobbling stack of empty frames, and you will stare at it while you pick at the fabric in the chair. It will take every ounce of self-control you can muster to not march across the room and straighten the pile.

THE APPOINTMENT

"How are you feeling?" They will always start these sessions with the most loaded of questions.

"Okay." Translation: "I'm flat. But it's better than being unhappy, isn't it?"

The doctor will take your blood pressure at each session while talking about his worldwide travels and his adult grandkids. He, like your students, will hide behind his laptop while you answer his questions. He will nod as you speak, and at the end, say that you need to make time for yourself. "Part of being happy is living a happy life."

You'll cry at every visit. Your crying may not make sense to you. Your rational mind won't be able to make sense of it.

Tears are for mourning. At least, that's what you were raised to believe. It is reasonable to cry when someone is gone. *People expect it.* "Oh she's so strong, he's so brave," they say of the stoic at funerals. They put themselves in the griever's shoes and remark, "I would be a wreck," or "I wouldn't be able to hold it together," or "I can't imagine what he's feeling," or "I can't imagine what she's going through."

You will hold this tenet as a personal truth. You can only cry at funerals. Openly cry, that is. Granted, you can dab your eyes at weddings and smile through tears at the end of a romantic comedy, but the broken voice, the swollen nose, the ugly, ugly transformation of your entire face? That can only happen when mourning the loss of a loved one.

The first time you remember your mother crying was at her grandmother's funeral. She crumbled in front of the casket like tissue paper, remember? Her thin shoulders sinking into her older sister? You remember that, right? How about twenty-five years later when your own grandmother dies and your younger sister falls into you the same way? Their crying, their mourning, will paralyze them. That's okay, though. It's supposed to. Funerals, remember, are made for that. But meeting with doctors? Certainly not.

You need to change your mindset. Think of it this way: you sneeze when you need to, and nobody questions it. It's a natural way of relieving irritation from the nose. It's self-preservation, really. If you didn't sneeze, then you wouldn't clear your nasal passage of germs and obstructions, and illness would settle in quickly and unapologetically. Think of crying the same way, except the illness is in your mind. It burrows in there comfortably, an unwelcome house guest, and leaves you burdened with extra work and exhausting responsibilities. You suppress the crying because there is no social equivalent to covering your nose when you sneeze.

Stop holding in the tears. Remember, growing up, when your best friend said, "If you hold in your sneeze, your eyes will pop out"?

Imagine what could pop if you don't cry. Just imagine.

THE ASSESSMENT AND DIAGNOSIS

Be prepared for a lot of questions, many personal questions that you will hate, coming from a stranger who is sitting behind a desk, behind a notebook, holding a pen and looking hungry.

They will all zero in on different symptoms, choosing their favorites first, and then working down the list:

Racing thoughts? Panic? Sweating or stammering in nervous situations?

Lethargic? Unmotivated? Sleep too much? Not enough? Thoughts of harming yourself or others?

Hearing voices or seeing things that aren't there?

Consuming copious amounts of alcohol and collecting sex partners as though they were Beanie Babies?

Are you smoking? Doing drugs? Do you wear a seatbelt when you drive? Do you lock your front door?

How much do you work? How often do you leave your house?

The first doctor will diagnose you with generalized anxiety disorder and depression. Her explanation is colorful, albeit a little ridiculous: "You treat every stressor in your life like it's a wooly mammoth that just appeared at the entrance of your cave."

You'll ask about the depression.

"Constant fear of the wooly mammoth is making it hard for you to live your life," she'll explain, as she rips a prescription from her pad and hands it to you.

The second doctor will give you a spiral-bound booklet (written and edited by the doctor herself) for you to read, annotate, and complete the questionnaire at the end. Think of it like a quiz in *Cosmopolitan* magazine, but instead of determining the best jeans for your body type, you're discovering the best label for your mind.

You'll answer how you feel at the moment, knowing that the moments change rapidly. Make sure you darken the circle exactly and use a #2 pencil, just like in elementary school. Otherwise, their scanning machine will spit out an inconclusive diagnosis. And the only thing worse than being crazy is being inconclusive.

At your next session, she will ask you, "Did you complete the assignment?"

Hand her the last page of the packet (conveniently, it will have perforated pages), and watch as she looks it over and nods. Wait for her to speak. And wait. And wait.

And finally ask her, "So what does this mean?"

She'll remark about your promiscuity, your inability to sit through a session without crying, your daily cocktail hour. Finally, she will rustle the sheet of paper around a second and say, "You checked off twelve of the fifteen questions. Eight is the minimum for bipolar." It's textbook. Open, shut.

You'll reread the questionnaire and want to ask, "But doesn't everybody feel this way some of the time?" Don't do that. You don't get to ask those questions. You are there to confront your mental illness and treat it, not to question or deny it.

The only doctor who will answer your questions is Doctor Google. Your diagnoses—generalized anxiety disorder, depression, bipolar disorder, seasonal affective disorder—seem incomplete. They overlap too much to be an individual problem, but not enough to stand on their own. You find websites with soothing color palates and cross-check your symptoms with their bullet points. It's this process that helps you conclude that what you have is, in fact, Bipolar II, hypomania with relapses of depression. You're satisfied with this. For once, you have an answer, even though the diagnosis will eventually be overturned by yet another doctor.

When you move on to the third doctor, you'll plop down in his chair and tell him you have bipolar disorder and you need a new medication.

The only question he asks you is, "How do you know you're bipolar?" You rattle off your symptoms while staring down the pile of empty frames that are still (still!) stacked on the filing cabinet.

He doesn't give you a quiz or ask you a series of questions. He'll take your word for it, take the other doctor's word for it, and update the notes in your file. Is that what you've become to them? A number in a database, reduced to a checklist of items?

After that, you will disappear for a while. You're an introvert, so it's easy for you to avoid making plans with others, intense social situations, and feeling lonely when you go three weekends in a row without any human interaction beyond the mailman and the clerk at the gas station. When you do need attention, you will seek it out in social media, responses and posts enough to sustain you.

Regardless, you will begin to teeter on the edge of losing your shit.

You will sleep more, feel exhausted, feel impatient with and annoyed by everyone, everything, even your pets. Even yourself.

This will be a darker bout of depression, the darkest in a while. Darker than you can ever remember. You will be buried so deep that when the mania finally does snatch you back to the surface and into the sky, you will soar along happily, surging with energy, knowing it won't last, knowing it can't last. Mania will look different each time she arrives at your door.

THE TREATMENT

The goal will be balance and stabilization. Your treatment will either focus on behavior changes, prescription drugs, or a combination of the two.

Your therapist will tell you, "The first thing you need to do is get sober."

Your resistance to this directive will be physical. Your foot will move to the floor as you brace yourself for the impact of change.

You're not drinking yourself drunk all the time. She knows that. She does. Yes, she does because you told her. Twice. Say it again, and you will look like an addict.

"You're self-medicating," she will say, and as she continues with her explanation you start to sweat. It's just a beer after work. It's just a glass of wine with friends. On the weekends your mantra is, "Sleep all day, party all night," even if you do so by yourself. Isn't that your liberty as a self-reliant adult?

"You can't do any work until you get sober," she will continue. "You need to stop drinking. At least for now."

You will shake your head and look at your watch. Time is up, you will want to say, and that's okay. Go ahead and say it. The truth is permissible, regardless of the weasel word it's veiling.

There will be many prescriptions, even more prescriptions than doctors. There is no single drug designed to treat bipolar, so those that are most commonly prescribed fall into one of two primary classes: atypical antipsychotics that toy with your brain's dopamine, and anticonvulsants that are used to treat epilepsy, yet for some reason have been effective at balancing an imbalanced mind. It will be many trials and many errors before you find one that works for you, but when you do, feel grateful. Not everyone is so lucky.

The first doctor will prescribe you Celexa, then increase the dose and add Xanax, and finally go up on the dose again and add Ambien. Xanax and Ambien are to be taken as-needed (and never with alcohol), so those will hang out in your medicine cabinet while the Celexa continues to have no impact on you whatsoever. And just like that, she will switch you to Wellbutrin, starting the process from the beginning.

They will all tell you to get more exercise. Not easy advice to follow when you don't even have enough energy to shower on the weekends, and—let's face it—the occasional Wednesday.

Try meditation, they will say. It will help calm you, center you. You will sit cross-legged on your bedroom floor, close your eyes, and practice deep breathing. Your butt will go numb and you will wake up an hour later slumped against the dresser, rested, but with a crick in your neck.

For you, there is no such thing as a quiet mind.

The second doctor will start you on a multi-pill regimen that will cost nearly $150 a month to maintain: Depakote, Abilify, Latuda, all atypical antipsychotics, and no generics. You've never been a label person, but you will comply with her demands, even as the pharmacist balks while filling your prescription.

The doctor will warn you that weight gain is a possible side effect of Depakote. You gain forty pounds in three months, maxing out your body at a size you had never conceived of as possible.

"You just need to watch what you're eating," she will say when you mention it, then scold you for gaining too much, too fast.

You will leave her office in shame. It's the most you will be able to feel, the best fight you could muster. You will have no energy, no metabolism, no will to do much more than to go through the motions of a day.

Your body has become a science experiment, and it's starting to show on your face. A friend makes a recommendation: go outside more. If possible, go near water. The theory is that when the sun shines onto fresh water, it will evaporate and release ions into the air. When you breathe in the ions, they're supposed to make you feel better.

Well-meaning advice, you're sure. But probably not the best idea to suggest that a depressed person stroll about a shoreline, lest she fill her pockets with rocks and wander into the river, never to be heard from again.

The Depakote won't metabolize like it should, and it will begin to stress your liver. The doctor will lower the dose and start you on Latuda, a sexy new drug specifically designed to treat bipolar. The first ever and quite a breakthrough. She will hand you a stack of samples freshly stocked by the pharmaceutical rep and send you on your way.

Within days you will have extreme bouts of paranoia, fear so debilitating that you will sit on your kitchen floor with your back against the stove, and be paralyzed with suspicion that someone is trying to break into your house. You won't go outside after dark, not even to haul trash cans to the curb, and the bags pile up next to the house for two weeks after that. You will walk a loop to every window in your house three times, making sure each is double-locked. And still, you will sleep with mace in your bedside table, terrified of the moment that you'll have to use it.

You will start to see flashes of color, of light, flashes of shapes that could be figures, but when you turn your head, nothing. There won't be anyone there, even though you sensed it, you felt it on your skin that you were not alone in the room, that someone was hovering at your shoulder.

You tell the doctor, and she will increase your dose. Each time you go back, she will increase the dose.

Your prescription is giving you symptoms of schizophrenia, but you won't figure that out until you ask Doctor Google. You will stop taking Latuda immediately, flushing the remaining pills down the toilet and shredding the boxes into the trashcan. You will quit the Depakote, too. You will quit everything, including the doctor. Cancel your next appointment and tell the receptionist it's because the doctor is a quack and her two-hour minimum wait time is downright abusive. Wait for her to respond, listen to her smack her lips, then hang up the phone, triumphantly. You don't need an antipsychotic. You need a doctor who doesn't think you're psychotic.

Despite his aloofness and disorganization, the third doctor will give you a prescription cocktail that makes you feel normal for the first time since puberty: Lamictal and Lexapro. His goal is to find the right combination of mood stabilizers.

MELISSA GRUNOW

He suggests Lithium in passing and mentions one of his partners was involved in discovering Lithium as a treatment, but stops when he sees that you are shaking your head.

"I don't want to be a zombie," you tell him.

He will warn you to wean slowly off the Depakote. "Don't stop cold-turkey. You'll put yourself at risk for a seizure."

Don't tell him you already stopped. Even if he wrote a prescription to replace the pills you threw away, you won't take them. There will be no greater risk than the one you have been taking with each old pill that you swallow.

Eventually, the nightmares and irrational fears will subside. Gradually your sleep will stabilize. Your weight will not.

THE ACCLIMATING

Get a new job. You like teaching, right? So accept the offer for more classes, even if it means driving between colleges in rush hour traffic. Use that time to call your grandmother and talk in a way you never talked as a child with your parents around. After leukemia takes her from you, you will appreciate those long commutes.

Connect with your students. Laugh. Show them you're a little vulnerable, too, that you don't know everything. There will be opportune moments in which it is acceptable to say "fuck" in class. Yes, even if you're the teacher. Seize those moments. Make your classes memorable. Make yourself memorable. Do this by inspiring them, *not* by sleeping with them. Sane people do not have sex with their students, even if they are your same age and more screwed in the head than you are. Can you assume you have students who are screwed in the head? Is that fair? Go ahead. People have been assuming you're screwed in the head for years, and they were right. Being screwed in the head will make you more empathetic toward others, and that empathy will make you a good teacher. You'll see.

Attend a writing conference. Surround yourself with people who are like-minded in a different way. Notice immediately a woman wearing an over-sized hat and dark sunglasses, even though you're indoors and the auditorium lights are dim. Stare at her and wonder why you're the only one staring. Her get-up will remind you of the Joyce Carol Oates story, "Three Girls," in which Marilyn Monroe wanders around a bookstore in disguise. Does this woman have delusions that she is a celebrity not to be recognized? Look away, take a manuscript out of your bag and pretend to read. She's odd; too odd for you to tolerate.

Maybe you're normal and everyone around you is crazy. Or maybe, just maybe, we're all mad here.

Meet a man who loves you, then lie there frigid when your naked body touches his, chemicals interfering with your sexual response. Stop taking the Lexapro, but be prepared for emotions that you had been masking. They will be angry and vengeful.

You will relapse into fits of rage and bouts of irritability. You shake, you struggle to wake up, but can never fall asleep. Your skin is sensitive to the touch of another, and you feel like you have spiders crawling around under your clothes. There will be no consoling you.

You will rebuke his affections until he finally asks, "Do you think you should go back on the anti-depressants?" He loves you, but you make him nervous.

Somehow, through the fog, he can still see you, still see a person, and not an illness. He will stand in front of you with his head down, giggling out nerves, tell you in chopped pieces how much you mean to him, his face buried in your neck. Then he will ask you to marry him, and you will cry, cry, cry as you cling to him. You're unpredictable, but he's willing to take the risk. Love isn't reasonable, but it's real.

Your doctor offers to invite him to a session to explain your treatment to him. You nod, slowly at first, then enthusiastically, because you realize it would be nice to have an explanation of your own.

THE CURE

Myth: Your illness isn't real. At best, it's a condition, but nothing life-threatening that requires round-the-clock care or consistent treatment. It's inconvenient, like arthritis, interferes with functionality, like migraines. A day spent locked in a dark room sipping water, and you will emerge the next feeling like a whole new person.

Fact: Everything you feel and everything you experience is real. There is no magic potion, no one-size-fits-all treatment, though. There is also no cure, so stop pining for one. Your illness requires constant monitoring like diabetes, it can fluctuate with factors of your environment like asthma, and it carries with it an unrelenting stigma like HPV.

It can stabilize. It can go into remission. You may eventually luck out and find the right dosage to keep you balanced and make the right life choices to avoid triggers and relapses. You may only have to see your doctor every three to six months for a Lamictal refill, where he will check your blood pressure and thank you for coming in. He always thanks you for coming in.

Leave his office and drag your fingertips along the mahogany banister while you descend the stairs. Thank the stranger who holds the door for you, as you step outside and into the sun, and breathe. Feel healthy because you do and alive because you are.

"Live your life, life your life, live your life."
—*THE LATE* MAURICE SENDAK *IN AN INTERVIEW WITH FRESH AIR'S* TERRY GROSS

ACKNOWLEDGEMENTS

I'm grateful to the following journals that published earlier versions of some of the essays appearing in this book: *Black Fox Literary Magazine* ("Meng Li Sha"), *Temenos* ("Totally Normal Until It Isn't"), *Limestone* ("We're All Mad Here: A Field Guide to Feigning Sanity"), *Blue Lyra Review* ("White Spirit"), *Oracle Fine Arts Review* ("Intentions"), *Angels Flight • literary west* ("Kissing Ginger"), *The Nervous Breakdown* ("Marked"), *The Dr. T.J. Eckleburg Review* ("Things to End a Marriage"), *Solidago Literary Journal* ("Dwelling Place"), *Two Hawks Quarterly* ("Can I Keep You?"), *Shantih Journal* ("Fire and Water"), and *Midwestern Gothic* ("Train Gone"). Thanks as well to Detroit Working Writers who awarded "Lady: A Rumination on Desire" first place in the MSU Forth Genre Creative Nonfiction Prize and Rochester Writers who awarded "Silent, Stifled Love" first place in the Michigan Memoir Award.

Sue William Silverman, Sonya Huber, Jason Arment, R.J. Fox, Angela Amman, Ming Holden, Kelly Fordon, Susan McCarty, Tabitha Blankenbiller, Bryce David Salazar, Leigh Stein, Sarah Einstein, and Leah Angstman: thank you for your support and kind words about my work. You all are amazing and just rock my socks.

For my brother, Michael, who called me from Italy on my birthday when I was really struggling to get my thoughts on paper and said to me, "Just write. Just fucking write. Just tell your story. In the end, all people want to hear is a good story, and you're a really good storyteller." A month later, my manuscript was finished.

My appreciation for the music of Stevie Nicks and Fleetwood Mac that I listened to for no fewer than 200 hours while writing these essays, along with REO Speedwagon, Radiohead, and the Pretenders.

To Davey McConnell for taking the photos used in the cover design: thank you for allowing me to use your work and trusting me with your vision.

Endless love and appreciation for Janel Mills: my proofreader, biggest cheerleader, vault, sounding board, ride-or-die bitch. This one is for you.

My upmost gratitude to the Board of Directors and editorial team at New Meridian Arts Press for selecting my manuscript from the slush pile and putting it out into the world.

Finally, thank *you* for reading.

MELISSA GRUNOW is the author of *Realizing River City: A Memoir* (Tumbleweed Books, 2016) which the Independent Author Network Book of the Year Awards selected as the overall "Second Place-Nonfiction" category winner, "Outstanding Memoir" category winner, and finalist for the "First Book-Nonfiction" category. It also won the Silver Medal Award-Memoir in the Readers' Favorites International Book Competition. Her work has appeared in *Creative Nonfiction, River Teeth, The Nervous Breakdown, Two Hawks Quarterly, New Plains Review,* and *Blue Lyra Review,* among many others. Her essays have been nominated for a Pushcart Prize and Best of the Net and listed in the *Best American Essays 2016* notables. She has an MFA in creative nonfiction with distinction from National University. Visit her website at www.melissagrunow.com.

Made in the USA
Middletown, DE
18 October 2020